Issues in World Literature

Issues in World Literature

To Accompany the HarperCollins World Reader

Edited by
Mary Ann Caws, with Patricia Laurence
and Sarah Bird Wright

HarperCollins*College*Publishers

Thanks to Christopher Prendergast for his initial help with this volume.

Issues in World Literature to accompany Caws/Prendergast,
THE HARPERCOLLINS WORLD READER

Acquisitions Editor: Lisa Moore
Development Editor: Dawn Groundwater
Design: Acme Art, Inc

ISBN: 0-06-502265-3

CONTENTS

CONTRIBUTING ESSAYISTS

Mary Ann Caws, City University of New York

Mary Beard, Newnham College, Cambridge University

Barbara Christian, University of California at Berkeley

Susan Gubar, Indiana University

Stephen Heath, Cambridge University, Jesus College

Carolyn Heilbrun, City University of New York

bell hooks, Oberlin College

Myra Jehlen, University of Pennsylvania

Patricia Laurence, City University of New York

Shirley Geok-lin Lim, University of California at Santa Barbara

Christopher Miller, Yale University

Earl Miner, Princeton University

Marjorie Perloff, Stanford University

Christopher Prendergast, City University of New York

Catharine Stimpson, Rutgers University

Susan Rubin Suleiman, Harvard University

Sarah Bird Wright, William and Mary College

Patricia Laurence and Sarah Bird Wright

Issues in World Literature
Introduction for Students

The essays in this volume should provide a useful framework for your literary and cultural travels through the various sections of the *World Reader*. As you know from your own experience, the actual traveler will encounter different attitudes as well as diverse places throughout the world. As you read the literature and orature (oral literature, such as poetry or folk tales, as opposed to written texts) not only of disparate geographical areas, but of various chronological eras, you also will be called upon to understand mind-sets and cultural concepts very different from your own, and to express your reactions to them.

Also, throughout your college years, you will frequently be asked to produce clear and precise writing—whether in the form of synthesis, analysis, narration, argument, exposition, summary, comparison, or some other category. As you embark on the adventure of reading texts that have emerged from countries and epochs very different from your own, these essays will provide various critical lenses that will assist you in making your own assessments and cultural cross-connections. Ultimately, as Mary Ann Caws suggests, you will find yourself constructing and reading "*a* world" rather than many subsidiary areas and separate cultures.

Your instructor will most likely assign the essays in this volume one at a time in combination with readings from the *World Reader*. Several of the essays deal with some aspect of what is called a canon, or a selection of works gathered together because they illustrate a certain outlook or are intended for a unique audience. Mary Ann Caws, in "Reading a World," Earl Miner, in "Periods and Ideologies," Barbara Christian, in "Whose Canon Is It Anyway?" and Christopher Prendergast, in "The World Reader and the Idea of World Literature," all illustrate the formation of canons in their essays, and also show that there is nothing fixed about them; they are continually evolving in response to changing political and social conditions. As you may already have discovered, the *World Reader* is not bisected by a formal division into Humanities and Social Sciences that obtains at many institutions. Many of the selections deal with observations about the natural world (Columbus's *Journal*) and are oriented toward anthropology, psychology, and sociology. Others are literary in nature, or have been shaped by philosophy or religion. A substantial proportion of the texts have been translated, yet retain many of their original rhythms and figures of speech.

Marjorie Perloff in her essay, "Making Room for the Avant-Garde," offers an important look at the history of the avant-garde and its metamorphosis today. You will find her essay of vital importance in reading and re-reading some of the selections in the *Reader*, such as those by Gertrude Stein, Aimé Césaire, and bpNichols, which may seem obscure at first glance.

In "Place, Exile and A-filiation: Migrant and Global Literatures," Shirley Geok-lin Lim discusses the important literary contributions made by writers who are displaced, by voluntary or involuntary exile, from their native birthplaces. She distinguishes between place ("filiation"), identity ("affiliation"), exile ("exfiliation"), and what she calls an "imagined condition of being without [desire, anguish, family, affiliation of institutions and nations]" ("a-filiation"). You may at times wonder who you are and how you became what you are, or you may feel lost in other ways if you have been uprooted from you native culture and traveled from one place to another. Shirley Lim describes a more profound and complete distancing than you and your friends may have experienced, but her essay will serve as an excellent introduction to variety of texts in the *Reader*.

The literal act of writing, as well as its representation in spoken and written literature, is explained by Christopher L. Miller in "Speaking of Writing and Writing Speech: The Orality and Literacy of Literature." He traces the history of writing as a pattern of graphic signs from its earliest appearance in Mesopotamia and discusses the broad implications of the terms "literacy" and "orality." His discussion of the representation of dialects by writers with whom you may already be familiar, such as Mark Twain, Flannery O'Connor, and Alice Walker, is a valuable gateway through which you may gain a better understanding of texts that are more alien linguistically.

The composite essay on "Gender" by Susan Gubar, Carolyn Heilbrun, bell hooks, Myra Jehlen, and Catharine R. Stimpson raises some provocative issues regarding sexual stereotypes; their essay will provide a vital starting point for analyzing a number of the selections in the *Reader*, from the *Tale of Genji*, written by an eleventh-century Japanese lady, Murasaki Shikibu, and a major influence on subsequent Japanese literature, to Virginia Woolf's essay "Professions for Women." Woolf's work as a whole has had a profound effect on what might be called the twentieth-century feminist movement, as well as on modern literature generally. These five voices examine the use of the terms "feminine" and "masculine" and their meanings in different cultures as well as in literary discussions and the university. We discover that the definition of what is "feminine" or "manly" is not universal but, rather, culturally constructed. These authors point out that speaking of gender does not only mean speaking of women but more broadly, speaking of men, homosexuality, and even race, and they discuss the difference these variables make in analyzing a text written by a man or a woman.

We all look at texts and art objects differently. Mary Beard's essay, "Culturally Variable Ways of Seeing," examines the differences in presentation, representation, and reading, depending on our culture and surroundings. Susan Rubin Suleiman's essay, "Literature and Politics," may challenge some of your long-standing preconceptions about the separation of literary subjects and forms and the pinpointing of authorial motives. She demonstrates that a sentimental novel such as *Uncle Tom's Cabin* has a profoundly political mission, while the political nature of works by Salman Rushdie and Karl Marx is offset by many literary qualities. Both the writing of literature and the criticism of it may be considered political, to some extent, yet many political works have an imaginative aspect that casts them firmly in the domain of literature. Questions about the parameters of genre are thus raised by this essay, as well as by Stephen Heath in "The Politics of Genre." Again, many students have been taught to assume that works fall in some predestined way into such categories as "novel," "poem," or "play," yet there are subcategories within each of these (romance, mystery, historical saga; lyric, epic, sonnet; tragedy, comedy, skit; to name only a few). Moreover, some novels have such a lyric quality that they almost become prose poems, and a play may contain lyrics, songs, and prose passages. Heath redefines genres as "stabilizations of relations of communication," but insists that such stabilizations can and do have flexible borders. Moreover, a genre does not exist in a vacuum, but may only be valid when opposed to other genres. He quotes the dictum of the French writer and critic Maurice Blanchot: "A book no longer belongs to a genre; every book answers to literature alone."

This body of essays is intended less as a definition of current critical theory than as a collage of approaches to the varied works contained in the *World Reader.* The essays deal, nevertheless, with certain issues that are increasingly in the forefront of the teaching and reading of literature and orature, that will have significant consequences in reshaping college curricula, and that are demonstrably at the core of many political and social realities today. The essays are less a set of arbitrary dicta than a sort of collective scaffolding on which you, as a student, can assemble, dissect, and correlate your own ideas. Together with the texts in the World Reader, they may also be instruments of illumination and valuable adjuncts to the gestation of your writing. They might, finally, induce the lofty state of creativity described by Milton in *Comus:*

> A thousand fantasies
> Begin to throng into my memory,
> Of calling shapes, and beck'ning shadows dire,
> And airy tongues that syllable men's names
> On sands and shores and desert wildernesses.

Patricia Laurence and Sarah Bird Wright

Issues in World Literature
Introduction for Instructors

1994

*Fare forward, travelers! You are not the same people
who left that station.*

T.S. Eliot, "The Dry Salvages"

This collection of essays by specialists in world literature teaches us to care about theory as part of the teaching of literature. The essayists tell us that, in reading widely across cultures, the work-a-day vocabulary of the humanities or literature class needs to be reviewed, reconsidered, and redefined: words like "literature," "period," "genre," "identity," "race," "gender," "American," "Western," and "culture." Under the stress of comparing for example, the literary periods of British literature to Chinese, Earl Miner points out that periods of English literature are inconsistently defined and are based on ideologically different premises from the Chinese. British "periods" are sometimes based on presumed qualities (Romanticism); sometimes based on a century (eighteenth-century literature); sometimes, on a queen (Victorian literature). Chinese literature, on the other hand, is divided by the dynasties of the emperors: Tang, Sung, Ming, Quing.

Conventional terms that used to guide your teaching will undergo a certain transformation as you read and think about world literature. As writers voluntarily or involuntarily leave their place of birth to live and write elsewhere—like Kazuo Ishiguro, who left Japan to live and be schooled in England from the age of seven on—what can we say about notions of nation, home, race and identity in our discussions of literature?

We begin then by suggesting a certain way of approaching these essays in terms of your own thinking and then by showing how the essays might be used in your classroom. First, it would be fruitful if you read through the ten essays in this volume in order to get a conceptual map of the issues that concern specialists in the literatures represented in the reader. You will see that the titles alone suggest a reconsideration: "Whose Canon Is It

— DEFAMILIARIZAB OF VOCAB /CREAB OF NEW VOCAB
— NO TEACHING VOCAB /PRACTICE / CURRICULUM /CANON = NEUTRAL
→ IMPORTANCE OF COMPARISON

Anyway?" "Speaking of Writing and Writing Speech," "Periods and Ideologies," "Place, Exile, and A-filiation."

Secondly, we urge you to pay particular attention to the vocabulary
that is being "defamiliarized" or created by the specialists as they compare
literatures. You will return to these evolving terms again and again in your
daily teaching. For example, the term "political" is often applied to
literature nowadays. But what does it mean?, asks Susan Suleiman, in one
of the essays. Does it mean that an author is writing politically or that we
are reading politically? Since we are concerned in this anthology not only
with how students read but with how they describe what they perceive, we
will want them to be aware of what they mean by the words they choose.
A new cultural-literary vocabulary is emerging from the cross-cultural
analysis presented by the essayists in this volume.

Once you feel that you have a theoretical "handle" on the essays—the
concepts, metaphors, and descriptive terms under discussion—you will
want to assign them to your students. Since the concepts introduced in
these cutting-edge essays may be unfamiliar to many students, we strongly
recommend that essays be assigned one at a time in combination with
readings from the *World Reader*. Using an organizing concept such as
"Literature and Place," you could assign the essay by Shirley Geok-lin Lim,
"Place, Exile, and A-filiation." Since this essay deals with the literature
being produced by voluntary and involuntary refugees, and migrants as
well as immigrants, you might want to assign writings from the *World
Reader* that represent this varied population: for example, Aimé Césaire,
Louise Bennett, Vladimir Nabokov, Alootook Ipellie, Salman Rushdie, or
Czeslaw Milosz. As you encourage comparative thinking (and feeling)
about the terms "refugee," "migrant," "immigrant" (voluntary and involuntary)— geographical, political and cultural phenomena of our time—
you will find that your discussion of literature will be transformed. New
ways of seeing and understanding people, literature, geography, and politics will emerge from your classroom discussions. It is this comparative
thinking in which you voyage across cultures that will make your teaching
of world literature, a new intellectual territory for most of us, so exciting.

Some of the theoretical discussion found in these essays will be helpful
as you grapple with this intellectual and cultural flux, because it foregrounds the fact that no teaching vocabulary, practice, curriculum, or
canon is ever neutral. They are shaped by a way of seeing, a cultural
framework. Always being *inside* a culture, it is difficult to get *out* of
it—without comparing it to something else—through intellectual travel.

- TRAVEL, OPENNESS, ADVENTURE (!)
- PITFALLS OF ETHNOCENTRISM
COUNTERING ETHNOCENTRISM
EVOLVING CANONS
- FORMULATING A CANON WITH STUDENTS

As you read, we suggest that you store in memory some of the metaphors in the essays that may help you organize your teaching of world literature. And we urge you to let yourself go, to travel. For it is this spirit of openness and adventure that will most influence your students' reading of world literature.

The *World Reader* makes possible many "modes of imagining," as Mary Ann Caws put it in "Reading a World," through which students are invited to reshape their perceptions in their literary journeys across cultures and along the continuum of history. Among the metaphors she suggests are the weaving of tapestries and the construction of architectural paradigms; she warns, as the French poet Apollinaire did, of the danger of lassitude: "Take care, lest one day a train should not excite you."

Christopher Prendergast, in "The World Reader and the Idea of World Literature," observes that "As the map of the world is contested politically, it is also contested culturally," and he points out the pitfalls of the ethnocentrism that is natural to us: the twin dangers of interpreting the ideas and beliefs of another culture in terms of one's own, and of assuming that the values of another culture are necessarily inferior. There are inherent difficulties in persuading students to look objectively across time and space, yet the *Reader* contains a wealth of selections that may go far toward countering their natural tendencies toward ethnocentrism. Though they will find some texts entirely alien, they should be receptive to many others, even on a first reading. It might be helpful to begin with thematic assignments based on selections dealing with love, adolescent initiation rituals, death, marriage, loss, and other general subjects and gradually broaden their exposure to the diversity of material contained in the text.

Several of the authors, such as Mary Ann Caws ("Reading a World"), Christopher Prendergast ("The World Reader and the Idea of World Literature"), Barbara Christian ("Whose Canon Is It Anyway?"), and Earl Miner ("Periods and Ideologies"), consider the matter of the canon of works taught, which may be reformulated according to genre, gender, intended audience, racial or ethnic origin, or other criteria. Through these essays students should come to realize that canons are not arbitrary but continually evolving, often in response to social and political pressures. It might be possible to elicit a trial "canon" based on their past reading and then redefine it by excluding or adding texts, asking students to justify their selections on the basis of the categories mentioned above, as well as interest, literary quality, subject matter, or political, social, or historical relevance.

— LITERATURE / ORATURE

Shirley Geok-lin Lim's essay, "Place, Exile, and A-filiation: Migrant and Global Literatures," has a provocative and useful place in countering set notions of literary canons based on national distinctions; students will surely approach her essay, as well as much material in the *Reader*, in the position of Homer's voyager, " his native home deep imag'd in his soul." They might be asked to search for common themes in the diaspora works dealing with exiles in alien communities, such as those by Nicolás Guillén, Louise Bennett, Vladimir Nabokov, Aimé Césaire, René Depestre, Simone Schwarz-Bart, George Lamming, Isaac Bashevis Singer, Czeslaw Milosz, Alootook Ipellie, V.S. Naipaul, Salman Rushdie, and Derek Walcott. Supplementary assignments might be the correlations of these themes with biographical accounts drawn from newspapers and periodicals or reports on the sociology of exile, based on statistical data or personal accounts (here *Facts on File*, the *Info-Trac* computer base, the *MLA Bibliography*, and the *New York Times* and the *Times of London* indexes might be helpful; note, also, the newspaper, magazine, and periodical articles cited in Lim's bibliography).

An enduring focus of the *Reader* is on "orature" as compared with "literature." A number of these essays point out the fallacy of assuming that literature must be written in order to be considered "literature." Christopher Prendergast insists that we must "sever...verbal art from a fixed associations with writing" and Stephen Heath, in "The Politics of Genre," recognizes the importance of speech genres, of oral poetry, that "stretch through time to provide a remembering that is a constructive part of the very existence of the community." The many examples of "orature" in the anthology, ranging from the "Migrant's Lament—a Song" from southern Africa to the elegiac "Rara Iyawo" from West Africa, to the Caribbean reggae song "Dem Belly Full" by Bob Marley, to the native American folk narrative "Coyote and Junco," should provide an excellent opportunity to engage the class in performance and discussion of rhythms and vocabulary that are sometimes elusive in written texts. There may be students who have had theatrical experience; they, and others, should respond well to Christopher L. Miller's essay "Speaking Writing and Writing Speech: The Orality and Literacy of Literature." He delineates, very clearly, certain distinctions between the spoken and written word and the difficulties of effective transcription of the former and verbal interpretation of the latter. However, just as the essay on "Literature and Politics" persuades readers of the sophistry of assuming they are in separate generic categories, Miller lays out persuasive arguments for dissolving, or at least blurring, the border between speaking and writing. Students might be invited to debate whether orality, as a system of representation, can be considered a broad form of literacy, or, as an alternative, they might debate the effectiveness of oral versus written texts. They might then be asked to defend their arguments in a short essay.

The essay by Marjorie Perloff, "Making Room for the Avant-Garde," should be extremely useful for students in charting the history of the group phenomenon known as the avant-garde and demonstrating its globalist construction within the *World Reader*. Students might trace the linguistic innovations Perloff describes as characteristic of the avant-garde, using as texts the works of Aimé Césaire, Nelly Sachs, and bpNichols; they might also seek out the poetry of Susan Howe, Gertrude Stein, Emily Dickinson, Bruce Andrews, Rae Armantrout, Charles Bernstein, Lyn Hejinian, Steve McCaffery, Bob Perelman, and Ron Silliman and test Lyn Hejinian's statement, quoted by Perloff, that where once one sought a vocabulary for ideas now one seeks ideas for vocabularies. Students might be encouraged to reflect on the ephemeral nature of linguistic patterns, especially slang; being *au courant* has its limitations even as it discloses new possibilities of expression.

The composite essay on "Gender" by Susan Gubar, Carolyn Heilbrun, bell hooks, Myra Jehlen, and Catharine R. Stimpson should challenge students' preconceptions. A standard comparison/contrast paper might work well here if instructors invite students to compare selections by male and female authors which have thematic similarities, detecting any differences in attitudes or in the handling of language. Are there enduring conceptual differences between texts written by or addressed to women as opposed to men? Compare, for instance, the anonymous eighth-century "Hymn to Aphrodite" (goddess of love and beauty) and the "Hymn to Demeter" (goddess of the fruitful earth) with one or two of the Hindu hymns to Shiva (the Destroyer) or with Patricia Grace's retelling of "Papatuanuku, the Earth Mother" (the Maori creation myth). They might also analyze the argument of the selection from *The Praise of Folly*, "Sweetening the sourness of the Masculine Mind with Female Folly." Does the Wife of Bath have much in common with the portrayal of women by Virginia Woolf in "Professions for Women," by Alice Munro in "Baptizing," from *Lives of Girls and Women*, or by Simone de Beauvoir in *The Prime of Life?*

Susan Suleiman's essay on "Literature and Politics" should yield stimulating class discussion and some fruitful assignments. Throughout the *Reader* there are texts at the intersection of politics and literature, ranging from Thucydides' *The History of the Peloponnesian War*, the works of Solon, and Usama ibn Munqidh's *The Book of Reflections: A Muslim View of the Crusaders* to the *Oral Epic of the Ghana Empire*, Castiglione's *Book of the Courtier*, Dr. Martin Luther King's "Washington Monument Address," and Jonathan Swift's "A Modest Proposal." An essay assignment might call for discussion of the literary qualities of such political discourse (including rhetorical strategies, metaphors, imagery, prosody, and so on). Students might, alternatively, search for political argument in such literary works as the *Epic of Gilgamesh*, the *Iliad*, the *Odyssey*, the *Tale of the Heike*, Dante's *Divine Comedy*, Milton's *Paradise Lost*, Ibsen's *Wild Duck*, or Kafka's "*Metamorphosis*."

These essays included here all point to the fact that, as Earl Miner observes, long-standing conditions and conventions of literature are shifting. Diverse canons are evolving, along with new approaches to gender and genre, class and race, periods and ideology, orature and literature. We read, as Mary Ann Caws suggests, "*a* world" rather than what we formerly construed as "our world" or "our country." A narrowly circumscribed corpus of tests has given way to one inclusive of many continents and many centuries. The instructor is free to devise wide-ranging syllabi that include works once difficult to obtain or little known; his or her vision should be enlarged accordingly. The essays in the present volume reinforce, in both theoretical and practical ways, the multicultural concepts embodied in the *World Reader*.

Christopher Prendergast

The World Reader and the Idea of World Literature

World literature is different things to different people. Consequently, collecting works for a "world reader" raises questions about the separateness and "situated-ness" of beliefs and definitions of literature in different cultures. This essay poses some questions: Does literature include oral as well as written texts? How does ethnocentrism come into play in our definitions of literature? What structures of power are established in society through writing? What is a literary canon and how does it evolve?

The basic purpose of this anthology is to give some sense of the sheer multifariousness of the world's verbal productions, oral and written, at a time when the "world" is increasingly perceived as both endlessly diverse and dynamically interactive. These connections within and across diversity in the literatures of the world can be said to converge on an idea of the utmost importance to the aspirations of this book: the idea of "world literature." The most famous version of this idea, and often the starting point for all discussion of it, is that advanced by Johann Wolfgang von Goethe, the great German poet of the eighteenth and nineteenth centuries, as the dream of a "common world literature transcending national limits." In the conditions of our own time, we might start to redefine the idea in terms of an observation by the contemporary Mexican writer Carlos Fuentes to the effect that "reading, writing, teaching, learning, are all activities aimed at introducing civilizations to each other."

This second version of the idea is likely to speak to us more powerfully and directly. There are of course problems as well as possibilities here. In the first place, such "introductions" do not necessarily constitute a polite get-together, though the spirit of mutual respect and understanding is an essential condition of them happening at all. The terms on which civilizations meet, both in out of books, are not necessarily, or even generally, those of equal parties to the encounter. Moreover, the effects of such meetings can range widely across a spectrum from exhilaration to anxiety and vertigo, as questions are raised, problems explored, and identities challenged.

Furthermore, insofar as Fuentes's view is a version of what we now call multiculturalism, there is the quite fundamental issue as to who actually gets invited to the meeting in the first place. This is a two-way consideration, involving both terms of the expression "world literature": it concerns not only who is included in the "world," but also what is included in "literature." Indeed, arguably the most basic—or at least the first—question has to do with what counts as "literature." For it is essential to remember that the idea of "literature" itself has a history. For example, what in the West is normally understood by it today (imaginative writing, plays, poems, novels, and so on) is a notion of relatively recent invention. The history in fact reveals a process of increasing specialization of meanings, whereby "literature" is originally equated with all kinds of writing, then subsequently, in the post-Gutenberg era of printing, with printed works, and only much later restricted to the notion of works of the imagination.

Above all, we need to sever the idea of literature, or, more generally, verbal art, from a fixed association with *writing*. This not only tends to devalue the oral tradition in the name of a specious fable of "development," but also overlooks the very real ambiguity of the acquisition of writing: at once an immense cultural gain, but also helping to institute structures of power and domination within which those who have the skills of writing and reading enjoy advantage over those who do not. Finally, it also overlooks the simple fact that, both historically and geographically, the oral vastly exceeds the written: the former is the most fundamental mode of mankind's self-expression.

These are issues that bear very directly on both the content and form of this anthology, most immediately, of course, in its commitment to representing (though inevitably in the paradoxical form of transcription) something of the vitality of oral cultures still active today in many parts of the world. Accordingly, oral material is both dispersed throughout several of the regional sections and also gathered together in the penultimate section to give some sense of the contemporary oral tradition.

This in turn brings us to two very pressing issues that touch upon the activity of anthologizing itself, especially on a global scale. The first involves the debates currently raging—and which will doubtless continue

to rage indefinitely—around what is called the literary canon. The latter
is itself a somewhat curious transplant, a term taken from religious discourse (meaning ecclesiastical law, or what the Church determines and
authorizes as authentic Scripture). The analogy thus implies both the
laying down of a law and the establishing of what is authentic, what truly
counts in matters of interpretation and belief. Its secular equivalent in the
field of literature is making a selection of works that will be held up,
transmitted, and taught as those most worthy of attention and study.

Anthologizing is standardly associated with canon-making. Conventionally, an anthology is a selection of the "best," and some of the more
influential anthologies even come to define what is accepted as the essence
of the literary tradition itself. On such a view of the purposes of the
anthology, an anthology of world literature would then be a collection of
a number of specimens of what, by some author or other, will count as the
great works of the world, assembled like so many heads of state to represent
their peoples and cultures (Goethe, in anticipation of his notion of world
literature, once referred to literature as a "common world-council"). This,
as we have intimated, is not, however, the view that underlies the principal
aims of this anthology, although in stating the exact terms in which this is
so, it is important to avoid easy simplifications.

For it is disingenuous to assume that in compiling an anthology one
can simply bypass questions of canonicity. The major reason why we
cannot bypass these questions is simple: selection of some kind or another
is inevitable; we cannot read everything and will want some guiding
principles, a kind of map, in helping us make our choices. A map, however,
is not the same as a museum (indeed some museums are now making efforts
to rethink their nature and function). More important is the point that, if
selection is inevitable, selections are human creations and generally reflect
the pressure of the present moment and its own particular play of interests
on a spectrum from the personal to the institutional. In turn, the valued
or endorsed selections can rapidly congeal into an image of *the* tradition,
thus overlooking or suppressing the vital point that *the* tradition is always
a selective tradition. It supplies an edited version of the past, which, when
critically examined, is defined to some considerable extent by what it has
forgotten, excluded, or downgraded (a key example, which this anthology
seeks to redress, is the representation of women writers).

We need to remain as conscious as possible of the processes that go
in the making of a canon, bearing in mind that, while they can be readily
simplified in the cut and thrust of polemical debate, the processes in

question are in fact extremely complex. It is not that canons, in the sense of valued selections, will disappear, but rather that they will be insistently and continually a matter of debate and subject to rapid changes more than in the past. In a society such as ours it makes increasingly less sense to believe in a settled "community" of texts, still less to treat them as quasi sacred. By the same token, it makes little sense to say that given individuals "belong" to a culture defined as a particular set of books. What may perhaps disappear is less the substantive argument about what we diversely value than the name "canon" itself, since the analogy from Biblical studies is not very useful and in some ways preemptively shapes some of the key aspects of the debate.

Ethnocentrism

A second and closely related issue that anthologizing, especially on a global scale, dramatically puts in play is what, originally in anthropology but now generalized into everyday discourse, is called "ethnocentrism." Broadly speaking, ethnocentrism carries two interrelated senses, connected with the business of interpreting and evaluating other cultures. The term refers first to the act of interpreting the ideas and beliefs of one culture in the terms and categories of one's own. The implied injunction here it to try to see and understand a culture in its own terms. It is prudent to begin here by acknowledging that following this injunction is not straightforward. For there are problems both logical and psychological in "understanding" other cultures. Thus, however generously endowed our capacities for imagining "otherness," we can never get fully inside the skin of another culture by virtue of the fact of not being a member of it, above all at the culture's deepest experiential levels, which are often unarticulated. Furthermore, if by definition we cannot have the insider's view, nor can

situated-
ness

we have the fully objective view. We are all situated beings, and this situatedness—historical, cultural, linguistic, and so on—both produces and limits the terms of our understanding. No one can see the world from the point of view of the world.

NB

This does not mean that cultures are so utterly different from one another that there can be no "translation" or conversation (that they cannot "meet," to repeat Fuentes's term). The point is not that we cannot understand other cultures at all, but that understanding them is not necessarily *easy*. Rather it demands complex forms of attention at once within and against the grain of our own assumptions. Thus, to return from these general considerations to our own project, "world literature" will clearly be a different thing for different peoples, if only at the very basic level of how you divide up and organize the material. Consider, for example, certain aspects of this volume. A geographical classification is essential, but the names we give to certain parts of the world would not always be the names other peoples give to the (the "Middle East" and the "Far East" are so only from the point of view of the West). Or take the question of historical periodization: terms like "medieval" and "modern" either do not travel at all, or if so, in a very uneven way (consider, for instance, the cases of India and Japan, neither of which fits into the Western system of periodizing categories). Finally, take the category of literary "genre." A uniform or even a simplified system for generic naming of the diverse literatures of the world can produce serious distortions and errors of understanding. In addition, it can raise sensitive issues of cultural politics: for instance, the novel (which we might be inclined to see now as a natural and universal genre) is not only a recent creation historically, but in its export (on the back of colonialism) to other parts of the world it has been at the center of great controversies, notably in Africa.

The second meaning of "ethnocentrism" has to do with values, and, crudely, refers to the (often unconscious) habit of assuming the superiority of one's own culture over others. This can occur anywhere, anytime. During the T'ang dynasty in China writers were classified according to four groups, in descending order of importance: official poets (male literati who had passed the civil service examination), priests, women, and barbarians (for which there were four designations—north, south, east and west). An anthology of world literature will by its very nature be devoted to resisting these habits of thought and modes of classification. Even here there are potential traps. For example, there is the logical paradox that, if in the name of anti-ethnocentrism we reject the notion of cultural superiority, then the consequent valuing of pluralism and tolerance must mean that we consider pluralist and tolerant cultures superior to antipluralist and intolerant ones.

Where the cruder forms of ethnocentrism are concerned, the sixteenth-century French writer Michel de Montaigne made the essential point wisely and well in the essay "Of Cannibals" included here in the Early Modern Europe section: "—each man calls barbarism whatever is not his own practice; for it seems we have no other test of truth and reason than the example and pattern of the opinions and customs of the country we live in." Montaigne sees the situatedness of belief, but also—it is part of the same process—sees through the fictions whereby one form of situatedness is readily converted from the pressure of ignorance and prejudice in the description "barbarism."

Finally, if the notion of ethnocentrism requires and enables us to address questions of cultural difference, there is also the necessary reaching for commonalities beyond the staggering diversity of human cultures. Without the recognition of commonalities, no "translation" is possible and errors of interpretation cannot be rectified. This, for example, is part of the point of the text included here in the Latin American section by Montaigne's contemporary, the sixteenth-century Incan historian Garcilaso de la Vega. As someone straddling the Incan and the Hispanic worlds, de la Vega's *Royal Commentaries of the Incas and General History of Peru* was in part expressly written —in Spanish—to give an insider's view of Peruvian history to the Spanish colonizers, as an attempt to draw their attention to the errors of interpretation perpetrated by their own commentators. This necessarily presumes a common ground of potential understanding (though many of the colonizers, as so often happens, chose to ignore it) and perforce leads us toward the discovery of other kinds of shared categories, preoccupations, and experiences. For example, most cultures seem to be concerned, in one way or another, with the question of origins, from the earliest text included in this volume, the Babylonian creation epic, *Enuma Elish*, through to, say, Darwin's *Origin of the Species*.

Though we cannot presume to see the world from the point of view of the world, a "world reader" nevertheless takes the world seriously. This, however, raises another question: what is the world (as distinct from, say, the earth)? How do you map it, bearing in mind that the "world" is not only a geography but also a history and a politics of both (to see this one need only look at the history of map-making itself: the science of cartography has been influenced not only by the state of geographical knowledge at any given time but also by assumptions as to what is "central"). Viewing the "world" as a history indeed has a name—that paradoxically specialized branch of historical study called "world history." World history deals in massive units of both space and time, and tends to group an otherwise infinitely heterogenous body of material in a relatively small number of "civilizations." There are of course different, and sometimes conflicting, versions of world history, but they are all concerned with tracing very general patterns and above all with emphasizing a particular theme: the emergence of an increasingly interconnected global system (sometimes called the "modern world-system").

The advantage of considering world literature in relation to world history is that it makes possible a very broad panoramic sweep over the material. From a world-historical point of view, it would be possible, for example, to classify the literatures of the world according to three kinds: folk literatures (that is, orally transmitted unwritten literatures), traditional literatures, and modern cosmopolitan literatures. These of course should not be understood as constituting a simple succession or development corresponding to the major divisions of world history (all three types still exist alongside one another today).

Moreover, in terms of the world's literary production, the relevant historical divisions are geographically variable (in the case of Japan, for example, the "modern" period begins only in the later nineteenth-century). Furthermore, the focus on literature (rather than, say, politics or economy) is likely to highlight certain historical developments as more immediately important than others. For example, if, as in one influential account of world history, a key turning point is represented by the date 1492 (Columbus's voyage to the Americas), where literature is concerned we might want to push the date of the turning point back some forty years to the invention of the printing press and the publication in Germany of the Gutenberg Bible (1465)—an event that dramatically and permanently altered the conditions under which literature was both reproduced and diffused. And here we would also want to bear in mind that China invented its own printing technology (based on wood blocks) many centuries before. The historical picture is thus very uneven and by no means unfolds as a straight linear sequence.

These, however, are questions of detail. The details, of course, matter and indeed have implications for the organization of this anthology. As we have noted, the historical divisions for different parts of the world are variable according to the specifics of particular regions and countries. There is a further and related difference in organization. In some cases we have treated certain areas and periods as single "blocs": for example Europe is divided according to medieval, early modern, and modern but undifferentiated as to country and language. On the other hand, we have broken down some areas: by country (the Far East) or by language (the Classical Middle East) or by region (Africa). One reason for this is pragmatic. We have assumed some degree of familiarity with the European traditions (what is sometimes called the "European literary system"); where the less familiar material is concerned, it seemed more helpful to separate out the material in order to focus in on the distinctive features of particular traditions.

Nevertheless, viewed in terms of patterns of world history, the fundamental stress that that history encourages is on larger and increasingly more integrated units. It also supplies the rationale for the major break within the single-volume edition and the corresponding break for the two-volume edition. Whatever the details of the arguments over starting points, world history strongly sponsors the notion of a pivotal turning point for the creation of the modern world, crucially involving the spread of Islam, a system of trade routes in the thirteenth and fourteenth centuries stretching from Europe to China, the commercial expansion of early modern Europe from the fifteenth century onward and the discovery of the Americas. We have tried to reflect something of these pivotal developments in the actual organization of the anthology by concluding the first part or volume with the literatures of these three areas (the Classical Middle East, Early Modern Europe and the Early Americas). This is in no way to elevate them as being more important than other literary cultures, but rather to see them as key moments in a world-historical story. The coherence of a story is always purchased at a price, in inevitable simplification and potential distortion. But there are also considerable gains, the most important of which lies in having some moderately clear sense of how literature relates to history.

This history has massive implications for what we can call the idea of world literature today, notably as illustrated by the concluding section of the volume. This idea naturally looks very different from the way Goethe saw it. Nevertheless, the idea remains relevant and active for us, though of course in terms of the changed conditions that in turn have changed and transformed it. To speak of world literature today is to do so against the background of a huge intervening history, marked by quite spectacular disruptions and displacements of populations and peoples, countries, cultures, languages. The main developments include colonialism and both its postcolonial and neocolonial aftermaths, waves of emigration on a global scale, spread of colonial languages to many parts of the world, the development of ever-faster modes of transport and communications technologies, and the creation of a fully consolidated world market largely controlled by the major powers. Though the nation-state has remained the dominant political form along with a variety of both new and resurgent nationalisms, the twentieth century is aptly defined as the widespread extension of the modern world-system.

We refer to this phenomenon, in the title of the concluding section, as boundary crossing. This is of course not in itself a new phenomenon. Indeed the very first section, The Ancient Mediterranean World, outlines a view of that world as permeable multiple crossings of cultural and geographical boundaries. Even in a culture as "closed" as the world of medieval Christendom in Europe, Spain at least remained open to both Moorish and Jewish influences. What, however, stands out in today's conditions is the sheer scale of dispersal. The dominant pull to the West remains, now from the so-called Third World to the so-called First World (the labels are of course problematic). From the point of view of literary developments, a key aspect of these processes has been the spread of the languages of the former colonial powers. At the cultural level this has broken or blurred boundaries on a vast scale. English, for example, is now commonly described as a "world language," although a sense of proportion needs to be maintained here (only around 15 percent of the world's population routinely uses English in everyday life). Where literature is concerned, it is also important to avoid seeing non-European literatures in European languages as what has been called "an overseas department of European literature." Above all, if the historical pull of the connecting energies has been to the West, the full picture of contemporary literary border crossing reveals a centrifugal as well as a centripetal dynamic, pushing out as well as in. Finally, within the West, itself we can speak of another reverse movement; as writers from elsewhere have been drawn to the various centers in the West, there has taken place within areas of the West itself what has been called "borderization," meaning by this an implosion of borders subsequent to the explosion outward in the classic forms of imperialism, whereby in a country (such as the United States) "cultures and languages mutually invade one another."

All of these developments need to be taken into account in forming a picture of world literature today, plus one other. For a fully rounded and balanced view also requires a recognition of the continuing reality of local cultural traditions and initiatives. Against diaspora, there are the endeavors of those who remain at home. Thus, we may think of many parts of the world in which massive emigration and exile have been commonplace but which have also sought to find terms for engagement with what is given by birth and ancestry, often against a history of outside oppression.

To lose sight of these realities, in the excitements of a generalized cosmopolitan internationalism, would be to lose something quite fundamental in the charting of the contours of contemporary world literature. This is even more so in relation to the local, indigenous cultures represented by the oral tradition. The latter reflects a very deep-rooted stratum of cultural life, and is one reason why we would suggest that the penultimate section devoted to that tradition should be read in counterpoint with the final section. But here too, along with counterpoint, there is also a potential relation of harmony. For the oral, however rooted in locality and custom, also opens up cross-cultural perspectives through common themes and traveling stories (for example, Homer's *Odyssey* not only finds an echo in the last section, in the poem "Omeros" by the Caribbean poet Derek Walcott, but also in the Russian oral narrative *Dobrynya and Kazimirov*, included in the previous section). It would seem that stories of the wanderer and the home-comer fascinate nearly everyone.

These considerations also encourage us in endorsing a final stress on the importance of connections across differences. To return once more to the words of Carlos Fuentes: "I found that culture consists of connections, not separations." The point, then, is that cultures are best seen as dynamically related and interactive rather than as closed, separate, and static. "World literature" in this context is accordingly usefully defined less as a concept than as a space crossed and recrossed by history, a space for which no stable map exists. As the map of the world is contested politically, it is also contested culturally. But where what is worst in the former comes out as an obsession with or imposition of fixed frontiers and dominant identities, the latter at its best is the exact converse, open to multiple encounter and the ceaseless transformation of "traditions." A world reader constructed along these lines is similarly a sustained invitation to undertake such a journey, extending and crossing frontiers, reading actively to redraw or to make for the first time a "map" whose contours will have to be revised over and over again.

Mary Ann Caws

Reading A World

A great American Poet once asked the Architect: "What slice of the sun does your building have? What light enters your Room?" as if to say, the sun never knew how great it is until it struck the side of a building. The Room is the place of the mind. In a small room one does not say what one would in a large room.

Louis Kahn[1]

The collection of texts in this *World Reader* has been conceived as a tapestry made up of many parts, threads, and textures, with many creators, and at the same time, a conversation between the experiences and visions of many cultures. What it demonstrates about interrelatedness, it also demands from its own readers: that is, a stance of openness, a spirit of adventure, a concurrent willingness to change long-ingrained habits of seeing, thinking, and talking. For the world is various, stretches far beyond ourselves and our minds, and is not—far from it—just our world. We are not simply reading "our world," nor can we be said to be reading, in any strict sense of the term, "the world." To think the first would be self-enclosed and arrogant, as well as wrong. To think the second is no less presumptuous; but to do what we can about it, in the limits of our knowledge and to the height of our desire, is at least to start along the right track. In front of a variously- toned world of writing and speaking and translations of variegated sorts, we can begin to read in some appropriate ways.

What is represented here is interwoven stuff.

Of these one and all I weave the song of myself.

Whitman's artful and large-spirited endeavor has become natural to us: from what we experience through reading and living, we piece together what we say and are. The construction of this world-to-be-read aims also at a largeness of spirit, personal and interpersonal. Had we but world enough and time.... We have world enough here, but always less time. In view of that, we have wanted a book you could take off with, wherever you were going in the world or in your mind, to read through and to keep.

In this multicolored tapestry we have woven, the unevenness of the textures—those knots and slubs—matter, as does the idea of the cross-weave. They must not, at all costs, be flattened into conformity out of some nostalgia for ease and harmony. We all have to learn to read and think diagonally, across the warp, to find the force lines of the original and of our own imaginations stretching out. Rudolf Arnheim, an astute psychologist of the visual, has written at length on the dynamic of the diagonal in our perceptual lives, how it provides tension along with balance, how it upsets the static and the solid. Our goal here is, without losing our balance, to refuse the solidification of things and concepts in their accustomed and pre-judged positions.

So we have to welcome the powers of surprise. The French poet Guillaume Apollinaire found, in the twentieth century that we now see finishing, a new epoch marked by "the order of adventure." Where are the great forgetters? he asked, for these were to be the new readers of the world, new and old. Unhampered by the past, they were to be free to read the present and future, as well as that past differently now. It is not that we hold, any of us involved here, a brief for forgetting; our conversation is made up of elements from the past through the present, of texts oral and written, ancient and continuing. Yet we do hold for a new reading of things both new and old, one that presents more vividly their individual textures as it does their themes. So we choose between translations, between renderings, in favor of what we know and feel. Apollinaire continues his advocacy of the spirit of the new with a plea for feeling:

Take care lest one day a train should not excite you.

We have to develop, all of us, the ability to be moved by something beyond ourselves and our culture.

The conversations we carry on with other cultures and their texts must be capable of transport as well as content. We have wanted to talk together, in all these different languages, about all these highly different things in vividly differing ways. From this difference our *Reader* weaves itself, actively, taking part insofar as it can. As we are all well aware, there is no way of being totally free of ethnocentrism, no matter how hard we try. Great as is our delight in diverse materials, we find ourselves occasionally queasy at their difference. The delicacies of one culture, it is evident, are not always taken as delicacies by another: say, the sea slugs that are for the Chinese the equivalent of our caviar. We have tried to keep a few sea slugs, those problems that attach to difference.

Reading such different material entails a new kind of seeing. Making things strange, as some Russian theorists advocated in the early part of this century, forces us to see them afresh; much of the *World Reader* will seem strange. We hope it will seem equally fresh: the "Canary Murders" could have been written yesterday, to figure on the "Murder Mystery Minute" of some radio station.

We are testing some available modes for imagining in these pages. The architect Louis Kahn called his plan for a Bicentennial Exhibition building "the Forum of the Availabilities"; similarly, you could imagine this entire project as the enlargement a series of regionally-based rooms into a street and then a city for thinking and for testing new kinds of thought:

> Architecture comes from the making of a room. A society of rooms is a place good to live work learn... *The Street* is a Room by agreement. A community room the walls of which belong to the donors. Its ceiling is the sky...from the street must have come the Meeting House also a place by agreement. *The City* from a simple settlement became the place of the assembled institutions.[2]

Thinking of this world we have constructed as a series of rooms extending out into a commonality and a meeting house, we have to remember how the greatness of such a city depends on its willingness to make new contracts and new agreements, keeping its collective mind "open to new realizations" - thus our collective attitude toward the establishing and upkeep of the construction we have been involved in here, with its renewable imagining of new availabilities, always making room. None of us believes in the text as something to be stuck on the wall, flat, finalized, and terminally boring because it is rendered in only one way; it is, rather, a rounded object and a fascinating subject precisely in its variousness.

This project shares something with the oral literature, the orature so liberally included here. As Edmond Leach says of the oral tradition, "it is variable, subject to human memory however aided by mnemonics, discontinuous, selective, and affected by feedback from audiences. It would encourage its transmitters to invent and to add interpretations."[3] One of the most challenging elements of the oral tradition is the way it weaves back and forth with the written text. As Arthur Waley says in his introduction to his translations of Confucius's *Analects,* we must not make too neat a distinction between the two traditions in societies where both exist.

> Wherever texts exist at all, even if they are accessible only to a small minority, the two sorts of tradition are bound to infiltrate one another. A Mongol peasant who tells the story of Buddha's life may have learnt most of the episodes orally from other members of the tribe, who also learnt most of them orally. But he may very well have learnt other episodes from a Lama who has read them in a book. And the same Lama, should he write a book, would be likely enough to incorporate in his story folk-lore elements belonging to an oral tradition. A Majorcan peasant who tells one stories about the Moors has probably never read a book about the Moors or, indeed, any book at all. But what he tells could ultimately be traced to printed texts.[4]

Such an interpenetration of traditions in their vibrantly interallusive character relates moments, geographies, and ideas in a vital structure, opening onto a great expanse as it opens in too. There are a lot of different people here and elsewhere, and they read differently from each other. We want to be able to read like them, even as we know we cannot entirely.

In his recent *Lost in the Cosmos: The Last Self-Help Book,* Walker Percy points out that when Kafka read his texts, he and his friends laughed together at them. To some of us that may seem astonishing: the deep irony of Kafka's writings may seem in no way laughable. But, just as when we hear that the Egyptians and other people weep at a child's birth and laugh aloud at a death, our surprise can open a world. Astonishment reenergizes what we read and respond to. Our willingness on occasion to forget and forgo our habits, does not exclude our remembering what matters. "*Remerica,*" said a mourner eulogizing the musician Miles Davis, "that is where we live." Memory is active too, and chooses what it holds. In all of the literature given here in abundance, oral and written, another chance lies for us to listen and pay attention: in ancient Chinese, "knowledge" consisted of "hearing much."

To change the world, said Marx; to change our lives, said Rimbaud. To do one might be, eventually, to do the other also. Our ideal flexible canon works against the pervasive and pernicious habit of only reading in one culture, for one time, and for ourselves and people like us. Richard Rorty, in celebrating irony along with literature defines an ironist as "the sort of person who faces up to the contingency of his or her own most central beliefs and desires—someone sufficiently historicist and nominalist to have abandoned the idea that those central beliefs and desires refer back to something beyond the reach of time and chance."[5] In the postmetaphysical culture he sees as advisable, and not as impossible, there goes, along with the acknowledgment of contingency, that of relativity: "This process of coming to see other human beings as 'one of us' rather than as 'them' is a matter of detailed description of what unfamiliar people are like and of redescription of what we ourselves are like." It is, he goes on to say, the skill we develop through reading "at recognizing and describing the different sorts of little things around which individuals or communities center their fantasies and their lives" that does more than philosophy for freedom and equality."[6] For Rorty, literature is the prime source of this description; narrative is more useful than theory, and literary critics are useful as moral advisers, "not because they have special access to moral truth but because they have been around. They have read more books and are thus in a better position not to get trapped in the vocabulary of any single book." They can, he believes, fit antithetical and oppositional elements into a mosaic of equilibrium, giving us "a set of classical texts as rich and diverse as possible and performing redescriptions" in ways which will enlarge the canon...suggesting ways in which the tensions within this canon may be eased—or, where necessary, sharpened."[7]

Believing that reading and creation are intimately linked, we entertain the positive notion that these gathered perceptions will lead to an opening of perspective, a strengthening of collective outlook, the ongoing of a conversation. If "by our means," says Virginia Woolf in her essay "How Should One Read a Book?" "books were to become stronger, richer and more varied, that would be an end worth reaching." But, as Woolf continues, it becomes clear that even the practice of reading is a good in itself, were it to be for no end at all. She concludes on a dream of the Day of Judgment, when "the great conquerors and lawyers and statesmen come to receive their rewards—their crowns, their laurels, their names carved indelibly upon imperishable marble." Then, in a switch to the collective and the personal, she concludes that the Almighty will say, and "not without a certain envy, when He sees us coming with our books under our arms, 'Look, these need no reward. We have nothing to give them here. They have loved reading.' "[8]

NOTES

1. Louis Kahn, "Definitions of Urban Architecture" for the exhibition, "City/2", Philadelphia Museum of Art, 1971, prepared by David De Long.

2. *Ibid.* That the building should have remained unbuilt in no way subtracts from his notion.

3. Edmond Leach, "Fishing for Men on the Edge of the Wilderness," in, *The Literary Guide to the Bible,* Robert Alter and Frank Kermode, eds., (Cambridge, Mass.: Harvard University Press, 1987), p. 589.

4. Arthur Waley, trans., *The Analects of Confucius* (New York: Vintage, 1989), p. 51.

5. Richard Rorty, *Contingency, Irony, and Solidarity* (New York: Cambridge University Press, 1989), pp. xv-xvi.

6. *Ibid,* pp. 93-4.

7. *Ibid,* pp. 81-82.

8. Virginia Woolf, *The Second Common Reader* (New York: Harcourt Brace, 1960), p. 245.

Barbara Christian

Whose Canon Is It Anyway?

Terms like "canonicity," "political correctness," and
"multiculturalism," have entered the conversation sur-
rounding world literature. The canon, a group of select
texts studied in the schools in a certain society, is not
etched in stone; rather, it is tied to a particular culture's
sense of what is philosophically, politically, and aesthet-
ically important. What is considered worthy of study,
that is, a canon, is constructed by a society.

In the last five years, issues of canonicity, political correctness, and multiculturalism have been hotly debated in the American popular media as well
as in intellectual and academic journals. The debate is often presented as
two-sided, with the "pure intellectuals" defending standards on one side
and the "politicos" insisting on social justice on the other side.[1]

The intellectuals clam that the politicos are not concerned with
intellectual excellence and are bending to political pressure. The politicos
insist that there is no such thing as a universal or objective standard and
the pure intellectuals are primarily concerned with maintaining their
cultural dominance.[2] Such a two-sided, simplistic presentation of the
debate has had the effect of distorting the character of its participants.

The word "canon" is an ecclesiastical term that originated in the
Middle Ages and defined the sacred texts of the Church. Because the
medieval Church was a powerful entity in Europe and controlled much of
education, those select few who had access to knowledge of the canon held
a particularly powerful position in society. As education became more
secular, the term "canon" was increasingly applied to texts that embodied
the knowledge necessary to a particular nation-state in its project to define
the national character. Because the majority of those who had access to
education were generally of the privileged class, a knowledge of these texts
indicated one's position in a particular society. In the nineteenth century
as education became more available to the middle classes in nation-states
like England, thinkers such as the middle-class poet and essayist Matthew

Arnold, in his famous work *Culture and Anarchy* (1859) would attempt to redefine "culture" according to a more democratic standard. For Arnold, the cultured person is the one who transcends the limitations of his class and caste so as to become "human." "No longer belonging to any of society's actual segments, [he] can stand above the spectrum of warring factions, dispassionately appraising, balancing, stabilizing and renewing."[3] An acquisition of culture had much to do with a knowledge of the "best" of the national culture, those texts that exemplified the good and the beautiful of the national character and to which educated citizens, whatever their class, should be exposed so as to transcend the differences that might throw a nation into anarchy.

If one knows the history of Western education, it becomes clear that the particular texts chosen for inclusion in the canon, as it is now called, are not etched in stone, but are in fact tied to a particular nation-state's sense of what is philosophically and aesthetically important. Canons change according to changes in perception of the national character. The content of the canons, then, is decidedly affected by the nation-state's self-definition and thus partially determined by "political" as well as intellectual concerns. In fact the political realm and the intellectual realm are hardly discrete realms. When one looks at the debate in the latter half of the twentieth century about the "American Literary Canon" in this way, one can see why there is such furious rhetoric. What is at stake is the meaning of terms like "culture," "American" and "Western." The debate may also determine who is considered an American and who is not, who determines standards of the good and the beautiful and who does not.

American educational institutions have continually changed the content of the canon in different academic disciplines. There was a time when American literature, or more precisely Anglo-American literature, was not considered a worthy subject of study, since the only literature worth studying was from England. Now, however, few American English departments do not include a course on, say, the American Renaissance or on writers such as Nathaniel Hawthorne, Herman Melville, or William Faulkner. That shift in curriculum had much to do, interestingly, with the increasing power of the United States internationally, as well as with Anglo-Americans' growing awareness of their distinctiveness, of the ways in which their national character is quite different from that of the British. I think that most contemporary American scholars and teachers of literature would say that the restructuring of the curriculum to include

American literature, that is, literature written almost exclusively by white American men, intellectually enriched our educational institutions rather than diluting our standards.

One important result of this refiguring of the canon has been the increase in revered and respected scholars who study specifically periods of American literature. For the field was found to be so rich and complex that one could even focus on a particular epoch as one's main interest, just as someone else might specialize in, say, seventeenth-century British literature. Such an intensity of focus has generated an enormous amount of scholarship, some of which has greatly illuminated our understanding of "American" culture. While there were practical dilemmas, such as how to organize a course given the inherent limitations of time—an objection often posed by teachers who are, after all, on the front lines—because there was an awareness of the intellectual necessity for Americans to know their own literature, resourceful people took on the challenge of refiguring the curriculum so that today most students who go to high school must study American literature.

Since significant changes in the curriculum of American educational institutions have not only been envisioned but have occurred before and American educators have been able to adapt to them somehow—often in remarkably enriching ways—we should welcome and support a broad infusion of cultures that will let our vision range still further.

Many of us have forgotten or perhaps have never known that "multi-culturalism" as a term did not originate in the educational debates of the 1980s. The term was, in fact, very much alive during the 1960s when African-Americans, Native Americans, and other ethnic Americans in many places in this country demanded that their traditions be studied and explored on high school and college campuses. What many of the students of the 1960s realized was that, unless the knowledge of a group is validated by the entire society, that knowledge is in danger of being denigrated, misunderstood, even lost. What even these students did not know—and how could they when it was not a part of their education?—is that there had been black intellectuals such as W. E. B. Du Bois, at the turn of the century who had already been worried about the ways in which the American educational system denied blacks their history and culture and denied, in fact, all Americans a knowledge of that central element of the their history and culture without which, as Toni Morrison puts it, American culture is incoherent. For example, major movements of the nineteenth century such as the abolitionist movement and the women's rights movement, movements that changed the character of American life, could not really be understood without a knowledge of black writers such as Frederick Douglass and Frances Harper, or without an understanding of the slave narrative or the sentimental romance.

Because art is generally defined in the West as that which transcends temporal matters and is apart from, rather than a part of, everyday existence, and because, in contrast, African-American writers have tended to see their work as having to have a use in present and future worlds, African-American literature has too often been labeled "political" or "propagandistic," characteristics with negative overtones in the Western philosophies of art articulated in the last hundred years or so.

Because of African-Americans' particular history, the intellectual as well as the expressive traditions of blacks in the New World may be of particular importance to today's rapidly changing world, where heterogeneity rather than homogeneity of racial populations is becoming more and more the norm. Perhaps the history, experience, and culture of New World blacks may have relevance to those, such as North Africans in France, who have experienced colonialism in their own land but are only now beginning to contend with the restrictions and fears that are the result of being a racially distinct minority population. An understanding of the social and cultural effects on an entire society caused by the exclusion of New World blacks may even be of some use to those who, although they may be in the majority in a certain region, are beginning to realize that none of us lives in a homogenous space. Peoples from different parts of the world have always been in contact with others; now, however, as a result of Western colonization and modern technology that rate of contact has greatly accelerated.

African-American literature differs from many other literary forms in that it has for some three hundred years occupied at least two intellectually differentiated spaces at the same time; it has been both a part of, yet different from, the European-American tradition. Because of the history of African-Americans, their literature has, of necessity, had to confront the reality of different races living in a shared space, and what it means when one of those races has been and wants to continue being culturally, socially, and politically dominant, to the detriment of other groups. At the same time, their literature also celebrates, in fact has, despite "Western" impositions of ways of thinking about the world, tenaciously held on to culturally expressive elements, which are judged by standards as rigorous as any from the West, that are uniquely African-American.

The written word is exalted in Western societies as a mark of the civilized, one reason why African-Americans have written. They have written in order to explore, analyze, and articulate the ways in which the concept of race has been constructed in this society, and the dehabilitating, sometimes deadly effects that construct has had on people, especially but not exclusively in American society. Because issues of sexuality and gender were and still are central to the denigration of African-Americans, both female and male, and because generally speaking they have tended to be economically deprived, African-American writers have pointed to the effects of the intersections of the categories we now call race, class, and gender. But African-Americans have also written to express the forms, vitality, and philosophical tradition of their own culture, which has its roots in Africa and has been influenced by other cultures, such as the cultures of native Americans, even as it has developed in the cauldron of racism. As a result, African-American writings, whether they are fiction, poems, plays, or essays, have tended to be concerned with issues of social justice within and outside of the culture and with issues of personal growth, joy, and sorrow, with philosophical thought, morality, wisdom, and spiritual regeneration as well.

We have to resist the tendency to make peoples of color into a monolith,[4] and work to obliterate the idea that people of color make no distinctions in their own cultures as to what is excellent and what is not, what works best and what does not. Yet any devotee of jazz, for example, will tell you that Miles Davis was who he was because of his artistry as well as his political resistance, intertwined as they were. In other words, all African-American texts are not the same. There are standards, not always the same as those upheld in the West, that African-Americans hold to in determining what is the good and the beautiful.

The issue of multiculturalism is complex. I am sure that there are Chicanos, native Americans, Asian-Americans, Latinos, and South-east Asian-Americans who perceive the world quite differently from African-Americans, for we have had distinctly different histories even as we have all been gravely affected by the racism of this country. If those who support multiculturalism support it only as an opposition to the West, then our identities remain defined by the West, just as it says they are. Nor is Western culture as monolithic as it is often represented. It too has its differences and hierarchies, a paradigm we do not need to imitate.

In acknowledging, exploring, and valuing the complexity of this country, and of this world, American educational institutions could prepare their students for the world that is already here. We might be able to value difference as a creative charge rather than a threatening reality.

NOTES

1. For this formulation of the multicultural debates see: Troy Duster, *The Diversity of California at Berkeley: An Emerging Reformulation of "Competence" in an Increasingly Multicultural World*. Publication forthcoming.

2. There are many books and essays that follow this line of thought—too many for me to cite. Perhaps the most famous of these studies are: Dinesh D'Souza *Illiberal Educations: The Politics of Race and Sex on Campus*, (New York: Free Press, 1991) and Arthur Schlesinger, Jr., *The Disuniting of America, Reflections on a Multicultural Society* (New York: Norton, 1992). Even as I write this essay a new book on the topic, this time from England, has just been published: David Bromwich, *Politics By Other Means: Higher Education and Group Thinking* (New Haven: Yale University Press, 1992).

3. Mitchell Breitwieser, "Multi-culturalism: Oxymoron or Redundancy?" Presented to the Humanities Program, University of San Francisco, April 9, 1992.

4. Troy Duster's discussion of the multiplicities of perspectives among Berkeley students from different cultural backgrounds, e.g. Asians, Latinos, and African-Americans, is particularly instructive. See *The Diversity of California at Berkeley*.

5. Audre Lorde, *Sister, Outsider* (Trumansburg, New York: The Crossing Press Feminist Series, 1984.) Lorde's essays are primarily concerned with the creativity that can result from our valuing difference rather than shedding or abhorring it. This is an insight—one might even call it a theory—that African-American writers like Audre Lorde have for many years articulated and explored.

Susan Rubin Suleiman

Literature and Politics

The connection between literature and politics is undeniable; however, there is a difference between political literature and reading literature politically. Depending upon the reader, literature can be perceived chiefly as utilitarian—as political messages—or as an art devoid of political or practical consideration.

At first glance—and for some people even after much reflection—the idea of literature and the idea of politics belong to widely divergent or downright opposing realms. Literature is a form of art, designed to give delight and pleasure, and at its best to provide insight into the complexities of the human mind and soul; great works of literature transcend the particulars of time and place; they continue to speak to us long after their authors and first readers are dead. Politics, by contrast, is nothing if not bound to time and place; it is concerned not with eternal truths but with the here and now, not with the individual yet "universally human" minds and souls, but with the well-being of specific nations, states, and cities, (etymologically, "politics" derives from the Greek word *polis*, or city-state). In short, it is contrary to the very nature of literature to be concerned with politics, just as it is contrary to the nature of politics to worry about matters of style or taste, or artistic delight. Politics is about power and action, literature about beauty and truth—and never the twain shall meet.

Right? Not quite. For if we start not from abstract reasoning about what literature or politics "is" (in such cases, the "is" invariably stands out for what the viewer thinks it "should be") but from actual historical observation, we find that literature, like art generally, has always has a more or less strong and more less overt involvement with politics, and that politics has always involved—among other things—debates about questions of artistic style and individual pleasure. Dante, the great Christian poet of individual salvation (*The Divine Comedy* is about one man's journey from "the dark wood" to a vision of Paradise), was also a thunderous social critic who "punished" his political enemies by placing them in the more gruesome circle of the Inferno—and never mind about libel, he named them all. More than five hundred years later, Victor Hugo (1802-1885), one of France's greatest lyric poets, wrote some of his best poetry attacking the "tyrant" Napoleon III (elected president in 1848 in democratic elections, Louis Napoleon, nephew of Napoleon Bonaparte, staged a coup d'état in 1852 and took the title of emperor) and wrote several plays and novels in which he criticized the unjust power relations, including *Les Misérables*—of recent musical fame.

As for the political side of the equation, one has but to think of the way modern totalitarian regimes, whether of the Right or left, have tried to legislate and censor artistic activity in order to realize that politics has not been indifferent to questions of style. Besides its well-known book burnings, the Nazi regime organized shows of "degenerate art" in the 1930s to display the modernist works it condemned, while it spent enormous sums financing monumental architecture, propaganda films, and "good German" art exhibits featuring muscular young male nudes, smiling mothers and children, and bucolic landscapes. During the same period (and right up through the 1960s and 1970s) the Soviet Union enforced its doctrine of socialist realism in literature and art by simply not allowing anything else to be published or exhibited. In earlier times, kings and rulers were legislators of art and taste—think of the pomp of Versailles in Louis XIV's day or of Rome under the Renaissance popes. In our own time we can point to the political debates fueled in the United States in the early 1990s by the photographs of Robert Mapplethorpe and other works that certain senators and would-be politicians considered obscene. In a far more chilling key, think of the death sentence pronounced by a religious head of state against an internationally celebrated novelist, as "retribution" for writing a work of fiction that he considered blasphemous. Although the Ayatollah Khomeini, the Iranian head of state, died shortly after pronouncing his *fatwah* against Salman Rushdie in 1989, the sentence remained, as did the million-dollar reward for the novelist's head; several years later, Rushdie was still in hiding, protected by the police of Great Britain, of which he is a citizen.

If the connection between literature and politics is historically undeniable, why spend so much time and space demonstrating it? Because theoretically and philosophically, this connection presents very interesting problems, with respect to both the writing and reading of literature. Already in the works of the Athenian philosopher Plato (fourth century B.C.), the question of the public function of art came up as a problem. In

The Republic, Plato's major work, in which he sets out his ideas on the ideal state, poets are treated with extreme suspicion because, in Plato's view, they stir up the passions and give priority to the emotions over rational thought. Indeed, Plato goes so far as to banish all public presentations of tragedies and comedies from his republic (recall the importance of theater in Athenian life), and he even dares to exclude Homer, whose works were considered part of every Greek's heritage. The only poetry Plato would allow in his ideal state was "the poetry which celebrates the praises of the gods and of good men"—what we would now call didactic or religious poetry, or propaganda. Plato vigorously condemned the "honeyed muse in epic or in lyric verse," which gave people wrong ideas.[1] More than two thousand years later, the French philosopher Jean-Jacques Rousseau (1712-1778) would condemn theater and novels for very similar reasons, even though he himself wrote one of the great "passion-arousing" novels of French literature, *Julie ou la Nouvelle Héloise* (1761). In a curiously self-canceling (but also perhaps self-promoting) gesture, Rousseau wrote a preface to his novel in which he warned mothers to keep it out of the hands of their daughters!

No doubt partly in reaction to the long tradition that thought of art and literature chiefly in didactic or utilitarian terms, a new way of theorizing about art became dominant in the West after the eighteenth century. In modern times, the most influential theories of art have all been deeply influenced (whether consciously or not) by the "autonomy of art" argument formulated by the German philosopher Immanuel Kant. In his treatise *The Critique of Judgment* (1790) Kant proposed that true aesthetic pleasure is always "disinterested," divorced from practical considerations or emotions like desire, fear, or profit. It followed that the function of art was not to orient the reader or viewer toward everyday life or politics—"usefulness" in the ordinary sense—but to provide a space where considerations of everyday life could be temporarily suspended in favor of "pure" aesthetic experience. In the late nineteenth century this led to the theory of *l'art pour l'art,* art for art's sake, propounded by the symbolist poets in France, Germany, and Russia, among others. Since the late nineteenth century, there have been a great many passionate debates, among practicing artists and writers as well as academic critics and philosophers, about the proper function of art—in particular about whether art should be "committed" to political or social causes or else maintain its "autonomy" and be concerned exclusively with the exploration of formal problems specific to each art form (in literature, for example, this means the exploration of language).

Both sides of this debate have put forward compelling arguments. For theorists of "commitment" (one of the best known of these was the French philosopher and novelist Jean-Paul Sartre (1905-1980), who launched the term "engagement" in a series of influential articles published in the 1940s, soon after the second World War), the writer's responsibility is always to write for his or her contemporaries, not for some hypothetical "universal reader." According to Sartre, writing for one's contemporaries meant holding up a kind of mirror in which readers would recognize their "situation" (another of Sartre's favorite words, referring to the specific historical and social context in which individuals necessarily find themselves at any given time) and also recognize the need to move beyond it, "towards the future."[2] Holding up the mirror, in other words, was not simply a passive act of reproduction; rather, it was an active intervention, a call for change. Sartre greatly admired the African-American novelist Richard Wright, whose books, according to him, not only depicted the terrible situation of black people in the United States, but would also influence readers, both black and white, to want to change it.

On the other side of the debate the "formalists" have argued that the writer's responsibility, and the greatest service she or he could render, was to venture where none had ventured before in the use of language, to seek to discover both new territories of experience and imagination and new ways of representing them, A near contemporary of Sartre's, the critic and theorist Roland Barthes (1915-1980), defended this view with great vigor in a number of influential works published in the 1950s and later. Interestingly, however, Barthes (and this is true of other proponents of formal experimentation as well) did not necessarily discount the political influence of literature, or its relation to the "real world." On the contrary, he argued that *by* restricting themselves to the question of language, of "how to write," writers would eventually end up discovering the "open question par excellence: Why the world? What is the meaning of things?"[3] The formalist position, then, is not necessarily apolitical but envisions a less direct correlation between writing and politics than the "committed" position does.

One thing that both positions share, and which distinguishes both of them from totalitarian theories of art, is a defense of artistic freedom. Whether "committed" or "formalist" the writer ultimately must be responsible only to his or her conscience. Implicit in this is a repudiation of all forms of state or party control, whether as directives about how or what to write, or as interdictions and censorship about what not to write. The call for artistic freedom, while unimpeachable in principle, can present practical and ethical dilemmas in certain highly charged situations. For example, in a time of increasing violence against women (the number of reported rapes and domestic batterings, even murders, has gone up sharply in the United States since the 1960s) should pornographic literature, which some argue does harm to woman by encouraging a general attitude of violence toward the female body, be regulated or banned? And what about racism? Should a virulently racist or anti-Semitic novel or poem, perhaps explicitly inciting violence, be published? Should it be available at the local public library? Is "literary quality" the relevant criterion in such cases? If so, who will decide whether a given work possesses or lacks it? Or is free speech the overriding criterion, allowing for the dissemination of all work—under a private imprint if no reputable publisher will publish it? These are difficult questions, going well beyond the realm of literary theorizing. Thinking about the relation between literature and politics, one quickly arrives at the broadest questions regarding the legal, educational and ethical life of a society.

After this general discussion I want to look more systematically at the possible relations between literature and politics. For that purpose it will be useful to distinguish between two different ways of approaching the question. On the one hand, we can ask what it means (or what it has meant, for various writers at various times) to write political literature; on the other, we can ask what it means (or what it has meant, for various critics or schools of criticism) to read literature politically.

In the most literal and narrow sense, writing political literature means writing chiefly, or even exclusively, about public issues or affairs of government. Plato's *Republic*, Machiavelli's *The Prince*, and Marx's *Communist Manifesto* are all examples of political literature in this sense; so are any number of treatises, manifestos, and petitions pertaining to the social order, of which there is an interesting sampling from a wide variety of cultures in the *HarperCollins World Reader*. One question we can ask here is how the word "literature" is used in referring to such works as political literature. Clearly, they are not the same kind of writing as a lyric poem or a tragedy or a novel; some people would claim that they should be discussed only in courses on political philosophy (or, at most, on the history of civilizations), not in a literature class. This is one instance where it becomes clear that the category of "literature" has no clearcut boundaries or defining characteristics.

We might nevertheless agree, as a minimal working definition, that "literature" is what we read not only for its informational content, or message, but with particular attention to the way it uses language, the way it calls attention to itself as a created, constructed verbal entity. Note that according to this definition, literature is not only in the text but in the reader: depending on the way it is read, a work can appear (chiefly) as literature, or (chiefly) as information, or message. Thus the *Communist Manifesto* (1848), when read in a literature class, may appear as quite a different work than when it is read in a class in political philosophy. In the latter, Marx's ideas may be analyzed in relation to other political thinkers; in the former, more attention may be paid to his skill in polemics and invective, his ability to use irony, sarcasm, and exhortation in order to move his readers—and rather than being compared to other political philosophers, he may be compared to novelists like Charles Dickens (1812-1870) or Victor Hugo, who were his contemporaries and who both wrote indignantly about the life of the urban poor; or to Hélène Cixous, our own contemporary, who also uses irony, sarcasm, and exhortation in her feminist manifesto, "The Laugh of the Medusa" (1975).

Both of these classroom approaches (the literary and the philosophical) are valid and valuable; they simply bring out different aspects of Marx's work. One thing they have in common is that they both treat this work as "past history." Sartre would say that such is the fate of all committed literature: either it is forgotten, totally unread, or else it becomes a text to be analyzed, a classic—deprived of its power as an intervention, a piece of "writing for one's age."[4] It would be interesting to speculate on whether, or how, a work can once again *become* "contemporary," affecting the present in some essential way, after spending years or even generations as a "classic."

Besides the direct, overt, expository, or argumentative way of writing political literature that we have been considering, there are more indirect ways,—and obviously literary ones, in the traditional sense. Take the abolitionist writings (arguing the case against slavery) before the American Civil War. Some abolitionists wrote tracts and treatises, fitting into the first category; others wrote poetry or novels, hence one degree removed from direct argumentation. *Uncle Tom's Cabin* (1852), by Harriet Beecher Stowe (1811-1896), was an enormously influential novel which did not so much *argue* the case against slavery (though it did some of that too, in the many authorial commentaries on the action) as *show* the terrible effects of slavery both on the lives of black people—whose suffering the novel depicts in the most vivid and heart-rending terms—and on the moral lives of the white people who participated in the system. Thus the sadistic white slave owner Simon Legree can be seen as an indictment of the system not only because it allows him to torture other human beings, but because he himself is reduced to an almost subhuman level by his savage cruelty.

Uncle Tom's Cabin continues to be read today, even though slavery was abolished in the United States more than a century ago. This work too has become a classic. Does that mean that whatever political "message" it had for its contemporary readers is lost on readers today? Not necessarily, for issues of exploitation and injustice—against people of color, and many poor people of every race—are still with us. It is certain, however, that no reader today can read *Uncle Tom's Cabin* exactly the way its contemporary readers did: if today's reader finds a current political message in it, it can only be in a transposed way, by finding modern parallels to Stowe's nineteenth-century depictions. Possibly, a reader will see no current political relevance in the novel, but may read it as a historical document, witnessing the political preoccupations of an earlier age. Or else, a contemporary reader may detect in Stowe's portrayal of her black characters traces of condescension and white superiority (the subtitle of the book was "Life Among the Lowly") and contrast her portrayal of black suffering under slavery with, say, the portrayal of that suffering in *Beloved* (1988), a novel by the African-American writer Toni Morrison. Yet a fourth political reading, influenced by contemporary feminist criticism, would look not only at Stowe's representation of race, but also at her representation of gender: does her portrayal of female characters, whether black or white, allow us to understand about something about Stowe's preconceptions, or the preconceptions of her age about gender roles as well as criticizing slavery? All of these ways of reading, although focusing on different questions, are examples of reading literature politically.

Is it possible to read *Uncle Tom's Cabin* "simply for the story," or else for its use of metaphors or its "symbolic structures," without being at all aware of the larger political questions it raises? Undoubtedly it is, just as it is possible to read Mark Twain's *Huckleberry Finn* (1883) as a "great American road novel" (where the road is a metaphor for a more abstract concept) or a "coming of age novel" or a "buddy novel," without asking exactly what role race (Huck's friend Jim is a runaway slave) or gender play in it. A political reading of *Huck Finn*, on the other hand, might ask: How does the portrayal of Jim reflect white attitudes about blacks more than a decade after the Civil War? Does Twain's choice to set the novel in the years before the war suggest a certain nostalgia for an earlier, more "innocent" America? How do "coming of age" novels vary for male and female protagonists? Do "buddy novels" have anything to do with misogyny? Does *Huck Finn* differ in a major way from more recent versions of the "buddy novel" or "buddy film"? What do such considerations suggest about the continuity of certain attitudes toward sexuality or the relation between the sexes in the United States? Note that these questions do not imply a lack of "respect" for Twain's work; they do treat it as the creation of a specific individual living in a historical time and place, whose attitudes were influenced (though not necessarily determined in a predictable way) by his environment, and who may in turn have influenced it by his works, for better or for worse.

For several decades after the Second World War, the dominant trend in literary criticism in the United States was the so-called New Criticism, which was more interested in the formal traits of literary works than in questions of ideology or politics. For the New Critics, only those works that manifested the most complex and ambiguous use of language (which some thought was the sign of "genius") deserved extended study; and such study, in turn, had to focus pretty much exclusively on analyzing verbal complexity and ambiguity. According to those criteria, a novel like *Uncle Tom's Cabin* was generally dismissed as being too "simple" to merit serious critical attention. A certain literary snobism played a role here: since *Uncle Tom's Cabin* had been a huge best-seller as soon as it was published, it could not be as "complex" as, say, Herman Melville's *Moby Dick* (1852) which languished for many decades before being recognized as a great work; and besides, *Uncle Tom's Cabin* was a "woman's novel," full of "sentimentality," unlike the "hard gemlike flame" of a true "masterpiece." Today, the *New Critical* mode of reading has been challenged by a number of other modes, all of which are more self-conscious about their own political assumptions. The New Criticism, possibly as a reaction to the political interests of the 1930s, claimed to be interested only in the "eternal" and "universal" appeal of great works; from today's perspective, this claim can itself appear political, founded on certain unexamined assumptions (for example, about what constitutes a "masterpiece," or "universality," or "genius") that require critical analysis.

Some would argue, on the basis of this, that all reading, and all criticism of literature, is political—even those readings that claim to be indifferent to politics. In a similar way one could argue that all writing of literature is political, for every work expresses, whether in order to affirm or to criticize, and in a more or less self-conscious form, certain cultural assumptions: about what constitutes goodness or virtue, about "proper" and "valuable" modes of thinking and behavior in men and women, and ultimately about the "right" way to live life individually and in society. Clearly, however, there is a difference between imaginative works that deal explicitly with political (public) themes and *proclaim* their own political position (like *Uncle Tom's Cabin*) and works that on the surface are exclusively about private "apolitical" experiences—for example, most of the stories in James Joyce's *Dubliners* (1914), or a novel of adolescence like J.D. Salinger's *Catcher in the Rye* (1951), or intensely personal lyric poetry like that of Emily Dickinson or Sylvia Plath. Between these two extremes one can draw many further distinctions. For example, some novels (or plays or poems) deal with political themes but do not apparently adopt a strong political position of their own. The American critic Irving Howe has called one of the great nineteenth-century French novels, Stendhal's *Charterhouse of Parma* (1839), a superb political novel, because it shows how politics works—yet Stendhal's own position does not espouse any of the political maneuverings he analyzes. Closer to our own time, Simone de Beauvoir's *The Mandarins* (1954) gives a sweeping view of the political concerns of the largely left-wing French intellectuals after World War II—but although it is fairly clear that the author is more sympathetic to some positions than to others, one cannot say that Beauvoir puts any one position forward as the "correct" one.

It would seem, then, that literature is a continuum that allows for many gradations in the degree and kind of political awareness it manifests, and in the degree of distance it adopts toward political questions. We can introduce still other criteria and categories: for example, realist versus allegorical representation (George Orwell's well-known political novel *Animal Farm* (1946) is an allegory, in which animals do the political arguing), or avant-garde versus traditional ways of writing. Jean Genet's play *The Blacks* (1959) an anticolonialist play in the avant-garde mode, more difficult to follow than a traditional play on the same theme; but some readers may also find it more memorable for that very reason.

Finally we can ask whether, even within the continuum of literature, certain historical moments are more or less likely to produce overtly political writing. It would appear that periods of economic or political crisis, like the 1930s in Europe and the United States, or periods immediately preceding and following civil wars (as in the United States in the mid-nineteenth century or Russia at the time of the Revolution) and wars of independence (as in India after World War II and in many African countries after the 1950s) are particularly fertile ground for the appearance of a politically self-conscious literature, as well as for self-consciously political readings of literature. Are we in such a period now, after the major historical and cultural changes that have occurred in Europe—but also in the Middle East, South Africa, China, indeed the world over—since the late 1980s? Whatever the case may be, it is certain that the complicated relations between literature and politics will continue to exist, and be debated, for a long time to come.

NOTES

1. Plato, *Republic;* tr. Francis MacDonald Cornford (Oxford: Oxford University Press, 1983).
2. Jean-Paul Sartre, *What is Literature? and Other Essays*, trans. Bernard Frechtman, et al. (Cambridge, Mass.: Harvard University Press, 1988), p. 243.
3. Roland Barthes, *Critical Essays*, trans. Richard Howard (Evanston, : Northwestern University Press, 1972), p. 145.
4. Sartre, pp. 239-45.

Stephen Heath

The Politics of Genre

Many kinds of writing such as dramas, novels, sonnets, essays, chronicles, legal depositions, epistles, epics, and satires make up a literature. Such kinds, or genres shape our expectations of a work. However, genres are not fixed entities and they continually evolve in response to historical, cultural and geographical pressures and change. What is the relevance of the word "genre," this essay queries, as we move between literatures and cultures in our study of world literature?

Literature exists as so many kinds of writing: for instance, poetry as opposed to drama; lyric as opposed to narrative poetry. We read novels, sonnets, essays, thrillers, parodies, fables, satires, and so on; with such groupings both responding to actual literature and organizing its production and reception. To write or read at a given time in a given society is to engage with the current conventions of writing, the expectations of what forms it can take. Indeed "literature" itself, which once referred to the whole body of printed matter in a language, is now most often a term for just such an expectation, serving to identify a particular area of writing and drawing the line between it and everything else (science, journalism, history—all the "nonliterary" areas). What is at stake is the differentiation of writing into writings, the availability of a set of identifying types. The most singular text is never simply in class of its own but is written and read in relation to such types: there is no genreless text.

The classification into genres has provided the most powerful identification of kinds of literary writing. As a critical term, "genre" dates from the nineteenth century (earlier periods had talked precisely of "kinds") and derives via French from the Latin *genus* meaning "class" or "sort," a derivation it shares with "gender"; in Romance languages, one word covers both, with gender thereby inscribed as prime category, fundamental genre (some non-Western languages have adopted the term: Japanese *janru*, for example). The major source for Western genre thinking is Aristotle's

Poetics, which set out to treat "of poetry in itself and of its various kinds."[1] These kinds are distinguished according to object imitated and mode of imitation (Aristotle is concerned only with poetry as mimetic art): tragedy is the imitation in dramatic mode and epic the imitation in narrative mode of the actions of superior beings; while comedy is the imitation in dramatic mode and burlesque or lampoon the imitation in narrative mode of those of inferior ones. Differentiation can be made, too, according to the medium of the imitation: both epic and tragedy are in verse, but the latter has a variety of meters and includes spectacle and song.

Important here are less the particulars of Aristotle's treatise than its influence. In a complicated history, the concentration on poetry as mimesis was supplemented by consideration of nonmimetic poetry and the addition of another—lyric—mode to accommodate it; this giving the "Aristotelian" triad: lyrical, epical, dramatic. The neo-classicism of seventeenth- and eighteenth-century France and England, for example, was obsessed with genres as standards of decorum, as fixing proper relations between styles and subjects. The models furnished by the classical tradition were taken as self-evident orders of writing, no more than "Nature methodized" (to imitate them was to imitate nature). Correct knowledge of genres and their rules was thus a necessity for the poet and had its own poetic genre, with Horace's *Ars Poetica* as model and Boileau's *L'Art poétique* and Pope's *An Essay on Criticism* as key examples. Shakespeare then posed a critical problem: his greatness was acknowledged but his plays were regarded as "mingled drama," mixing tragic with comic elements in breach of genre propriety. Significantly, when this judgment was challenged, a need was felt for new genre identifications that would set aside what Coleridge called "misapplied names" and do justice to the "different genus" of the plays.

Generic naming indeed can be an explicit part of the presentation of works, including in their very titles: *Roman de la Rose, Isayoi nikki* (Abutsu Ni; *nikki* are personal, "diary" narratives), *Pagina meditationum* (Marguerite d'Oignt), *Essais* (Montaigne), *Narrative of the Life of Frederick Douglass an American Slave Written by Himself, Duineser Elegien* (Rilke), *Une si longue lettre* (Mariama Bâ). Not that such identifications should be taken for granted: genres are not fixed essences and these names need to be understood each time in their historical context and for the various textual effects they can produce: Douglass's work is indeed the narrative of a life but Ba's is really a novel (in the form of a letter); "Psalms" suggests a certain unity for a book that may also be seen as made up of a number of different poetic kinds, notably praise poems and supplications (the Hebrew title,

Tehillim, means "praises"); *Kim Van Kieu* (Nguyen Du) is known in English as *The Tale of Kieu,* with "tale" and its suggestion of folk simplicity serving to familiarize a narrative poem whose title is in fact made up of the names of its main characters (an alternative title, *Doan Truong tan Thanh,* points reflexively to its refashioning of an old, sad story: literally "bowels in torment, new style"). *The History of Emily Montague* (Frances Brooke) an epistolary novel, is very different from *Historia de las Indias* (Las Casas), a chronicle, personal testimony, and treatise in one, and both are very different again from an academic work labelled "history" or "historia" today. But then, too, what does it mean to differentiate so confidently, to slip works into this or that category—"really" a novel, "novel" as opposed to "history," and so on?

Historically, genres and concern with them are to be found throughout world literature, in all cultures. The *Shih-ching,* the classic anthology of early Chinese poetry, gave rise to a tradition of scholarship whose great achievement was the *Wên-hsin tiao-lung* by the fifth-century literary historian Liu Hsieh: Liu's interest was exactly in the kinds of poetry, and his study reflects on the nature of the genre before proceeding to a chapter-by-chapter account of the genres to be found in the *Shih-ching.* The palaces of fifteenth- and sixteenth-century Aztec civilization had "houses of song" attached to them, *cuicacalli* whose function was the strict regulation of the composition and performance of lyric poems (poems such as are recorded in the *Cantares mexicanos* codex). The oral poetry of the Yoruba people traditionally falls into a number of genres—*oríkì* ("praise poetry"), *ofò* ("incantations"), *àló àpamò* ("riddles"), and so on—strictly differentiated by linguistic and semantic features that determine their recognition and allow their identification in performance.

These examples of genre thinking and practice leave open questions as to what we are to understand by the term and its relevance for world literature, for moving between literatures. The dramatic is a mode of presentation that can be seen across cultures throughout history and thought about in connection with Sophocles and Bhasa and Zeami and Goethe. Sonnet and haiku are set poetic forms with a limited cross-cultural reach: sonnets are found in European- language literatures; the haiku is specifically Japanese but is sometimes adapted to other poetries (witness Pound's "In a Station of the Metro"). Elegy and *shishosetsu* come with ideas of both form and content: a poem mourning a death or meditating on the passing of a life; a novel or story aimed at producing the conviction of a faithfully chronicled personal experience (Shiga Naoya's "At Kinosaki") is an example). Elegy, however, also has a history that includes the initial use of the term in classical Greek and Latin literatures to refer to a particular verse couplet, and a subsequent development in which it comes to refer very generally to poems expressive of some mood of meditative melancholy; the *shishosetsu*, which has its great moment in the 1920s and 1930s, became influential throughout twentieth-century Japanese literature, beyond genre boundaries, creating something of a general perspective of writing. We could then return to sonnet and haiku which, while defined formally as particular verse patterns, are also developed historically around specific thematic concerns: introduced in thirteenth-century Italy, the sonnet was fashioned through Patriarch into the medium of a particular Renaissance version of love; originating in fifteenth-century humorous linked-verse or *haikai*, the haiku developed as the representative poetic form of the Edo period, meaning to express what Basho described as "inner sensibilities in harmony with things" but aiming also at a certain closeness to the city life of the *chnin*, the new mercantile classes. Both sonnet and haiku continue up to the present, but with specific thematic reworkings (including the late- nineteenth-century renewal of the haiku, which gives the term itself its currency).

A strong account of genre insists in one way or another on an intersection of modes and themes, as for Aristotle tragedy is a particular type of subject dramatically presented. The lyrical-epical-dramatic triad is thus a matter not of genres but rather of modes of enunciation, ways of presenting that do not in themselves involve any defined content. This can be difficult to grasp because the Romantic and post-Romantic elaboration of the triad has recast modes as thematically substantial, indeed as *moods* (so we often use the word "dramatic" with no reference to mode, meaning vivid, compelling, momentous—dramatic colors, dramatic events). Modes as such, however, belong to the pragmatics of language, are possibilities of language use; a genre is a characteristic mobilization of one ore more of those possibilities to some specific end: such a definition taking genres as a fact of all discourse, not of literature alone.

The Russian critic and theorist Mikhail Bakhtin talks of "speech genres." We use language to make individual utterances, but those utterances fall within relatively stable types, generic forms that are the condition of communication: were each utterance simply individual, *sui generis*, we would never recognize the finality, the *sense*, of what we were hearing or reading. These forms can then be more or less open to variation: patient-therapist conversations have greater plasticity than military commands.

Literary genres are examples of such speech genres but differ significantly from the basic ones of everyday communication: "the vast majority of literary genres are secondary, complex genres composed of various transformed primary genres (the rejoinder in dialogue, everyday stories, letters, diaries, minutes, and so forth). As a rule, these secondary genres of complex cultural communication *play out* various forms of primary speech communication."[2] So a novel will include a number of primary genres but absorbed into another kind of utterance which removes them from the immediacy of everyday life, catching them up into its own reality as literary-artistic event. By virtue of their complexity and their work of transformation—the playing out—of primary forms, such secondary genres are those that most allow for freedom of individual expression; an freedom, however, that is not outside but from within—even as it may challenge and defeat—the resources of existing genres.

If mode and theme and formal matters of diction, meter and so on are the aspects to which we look in distinguishing genres, we need also to think of audience and effect (Aristotle characterized tragedy as effecting a purgation of pity and fear). Genres, in fact, have been and are identified in many ways and by reference to a variety of aspects in a variety of combinations. Aspects that are crucial in the identification of one genre may not be so in that of another (for example, length plays a fundamental part in distinguishing the short story but not the pastoral poem), while particular features of this or that aspect can be shared by different genres (for example, a certain theme can be common to more than one genre). There are difficulties as to saying what kind of concept "genre" is and even as to what particular genres are, since it is far from easy to arrive at any definition that will adequately determine which works will or will not fall within a genre (other than by equating genre with technical form, so that the sonnet as a verse form is a genre or the novel as "a fiction in prose of a certain extent"—which makes for a genre that sets the early-eleventh-century *Genji Monogatari* alongside the mid-nineteenth-century *Madame Bovary*). Where neo-classicism assumed fixed identities, leaving it relatively untroubled by problems as to the *theory* of genre, modern Western criticism refuses them, leaving it very much concerned with such theory, finally stressing the looseness or fuzziness of genre definitions and perceptions. The search for features shared by all works of a genre gives way to the notion of groups of texts linked by "family resemblance": elements are held in common in the group but are not all present in each of its members. Thus no one work will possess features that can identify all the works in the genre; though some works will see prototypical, more centrally defining an others *Madame Bovary* has been such a work for the novel in a way that say, *Gulliver's Travels* has not. Conversely, no one genre will exhaustively identify an individual work which, to a greater or lesser degree, will be involved in other genres (beginning with Bakhtin's primary genres), will belong to more than one genre (Spenser's *Faerie Queene* is epic, romance, political allegory, moral treatise), and will be available for genre redefinition (Proust's *A la recherche du temps perdu* read now through gay studies as a charter text "in that most intriguing of genres, the coming-out story that doesn't come out").

The family resemblance account should not be taken to mean that genres have no substantial reality. To look at literature through genres is to grasp it historically inasmuch as they are precisely not "natural" forms or abstract categories, but specific sociohistorical operations of language by speakers and listeners, writers, and readers: orders of discourse that change, shift, travel, lose force, come and go over time and cultures. That there may be no statistically enclosing *is* definition of a genre does not leave it as some nominalist fancy, just some arbitrary grouping of texts by literary critics. As Bakhtin suggests, there is a necessary practice of genres whether or not there is any elaborated account of them: the reality of linguistic communication is always that of *kinds of utterance*. If these kinds are constructed in the descriptions and analyses of linguists, historians, critics and others, they are also practical forms of recognition: horizons of expectation for listeners or readers, models or production for speakers or writers. Genres, in other words, are *representative*, typical codifications of discursive properties corresponding to typical situations of communication and with typical conceptions of who is being addressed, whether this be in terms of particular subjectivity, community membership, religious adherence, sexual orientation, class position, or whatever (thus romance fiction today typically identifies its readers as female, heterosexual, working- and lower middle-class, a commercial audience). Such genre address, moreover *appeals*, is an envisaged mobilization of desire, holding reader or listener to pleasures that define her or his generic participation (the romance envisages strong heroine identification, release into fantasy, romantic-erotic stimulation.)

Genres are stabilizations of relations of communication. Necessarily conservative inasmuch as they depend on the reworking of recognized ways of making sense, they are also possible sites for a conservatism that turns recognition and reworking into regulation and repetition, into laws that are institutionally supported in one way or another; the prescriptive rules of French neo-classicism—unities of time, place and action—and the supervised composition of Aztec poetry are examples. They are conservative too in their potential to function as a kind of memory through the process of recollection they involve. The genres of Yoruba oral poetry stretch through time to provide a remembering that is a constructive part of the very existence of the community. Milton knows epic as a genre that runs back over two thousand years; *Paradise Lost* recalls Homer and Virgil and Tasso, rewrites epic tradition with Christian matter. But also vice versa: the Bible itself is read through and for the genre, so that the Book of Job is for Milton "a brief model" of "the epic form" (where biblical scholars today usually include Job among "wisdom writings," identified as a characteristic genre of the ancient Near East.)

If genres are forms of history, they are also, of course, as this last example indicates, historical forms, articulated within sociohistorical contexts. The generic memory the epic brings is taken up by Milton in a quite specific moment of writing, a moment that includes exactly this long-scale, transcultural imagination of the epic form and its models. As sociohistorical operations, genres are open-ended, subject to modification as new utterances change understanding of them (*Paradise Lost* is written in relation to a generic model that it then *newly* exemplifies; the epic is not an essence that Homer's *Iliad* first embodied but the articulation and perception historically of a kind of writing that Milton, as it were, makes up again in his poem) and as the cultural conditions supporting their continuation significantly alter (the development of middle-class industrial societies in nineteenth-century Europe goes along with a secularized, bourgeois culture which finds its meanings in ordinary social terms rather than epic and heroic ones; the epic loses force, the novel emerges as the new genre of this new world—prosaic, realistic, *anti*-epic).

Generic continuities are matched by discontinuities, memory by invention, in complex processes of change. New genres are constantly formed from old ones as additional texts with shifting textual practices problematize the genre conception or as available discourses are brought together into a different form of writing (so Montaigne "invents" the essay). Different contexts of reading or listening produce new or altered genre identifications as kinds of writing with little or no formal recognition become accredited as genres in response to changing sociohistorical pressures (so African-American slave narratives gain acknowledgment and are read as a specific genre from contemporary awareness of matters of race and identity and the recognition of history and the literary canon. Equally they produce new genres and generic transformations, as classes or groups define and redefine the conditions and understanding of their existence (so rap has emerged in the United States today as a powerful genre of young African-Americans' social expression).

We can grasp the politics of genre here as a politics of representation, with change and innovation implicated in crises as to who and what is represented and how and to whom. Typically such crises involve distur- bance of and resistance to existing genres from the perception of and appeal to a reality that the resulting new or transformed genres will help precisely to *know*, to bring into meaning. Genres, that is, are attempts to make representational and representative sense. Faced with the "new" world of the Americas, the European missionaries and colonialists experience some- thing "so extraordinary," as Las Casas put it, that their genres—chronicle, natural history, legal deposition, epistle—are marshalled *and confronted* with contradictory discourses of "what they saw," their testimony produc- ing tensions of "like" and "unlike," "same" and "other," and initiating a work of representation that carries through the centuries in the renewed practices of colonial discourse. Faced with the contemporary United States, Toni Morrison has described a politically contradictory relation of the black woman writer to the novel, necessary genre of the claiming of identity (its historical function for the middle class and then for other groups in the modern world) and, as genre, necessary to undercut in a deconstructive, dialogical refusal of the terms of representation it sets (the novel as formally, generically, representative of a specific subjectivity—bourgeois, white, male)—and its fixing vision of things.

A genre exists only in conjunction with other genres, is distinguished by virtue of its differences from those others to which it is related in what at any given moment is a system of genres. Issues of the politics of genre carry through directly from this. Bakhtin's account of genres as "literary" in terms of elaboration and complexity, as against immediacy and every- dayness, brings with it a particular systematic assumption of literature involving *secondary* over *primary* genres. The relations of these primary speech genres to literature and its genres, however, are culturally variable and subject to quite distinct terms of understanding. Genres of oral poetry, for instance, may well depend on and demand recognition of relations between the community's speech genres for which such appositions as complex/everyday or immediacy/mediation will be damagingly irrelevant. Indeed the very idea of literature here, its habitual confinement to the written, is part of the problem, precisely to counter which the Kenyan novelist Ngugi wa Thiong'o has proposed the term "orature," referring to all the kinds of oral utterances in African culture, poetry included. But we need cultural caution too when looking at the stories of a writer such as the Nigerian Amos Tutuola, whose works create a "written orality" that has been described as Yoruba speech using English words and that invokes proverbs, riddles, tales, and songs in a way that is not just some Western literary "playing out"; the works can be taken as "novels" but are in tension with the assumptions of that genre identification, and first and foremost with those of any primary/secondary mastery of discourses. To grasp—to *read*—such tension is central to the study of world literature today, to the reality of writings that exist in a situation of the extensive influence of Western forms and of the struggle for other definitions, new generic terms within and against them.

The politics of genre turns on the distinctions it makes and the hierarchies those distinctions readily support: between high and low, sacred and secular, poetic and prosaic, literary and nonliterary genres. To challenge and transform such hierarchies involves a range of shifts in perception and genre judgment, notably as to what counts as the proper matter and language of literature, as to what to *recognize*. The development of the novel provides a powerful middle class with a genre that seeks to represent the terms of its world in defiance of traditional genre views of the actual social life of men and women as fitting only for comedy or satire (the supreme genres are conceived as universal, expressing essential truths in abstraction from the contingencies of the everyday). Diaries, domestic journals, and personal narratives are examples of genres that recent feminist theory and practice has been concerned to accredit, calling into question the gender-ideological bases of existing genre assumptions (distinctions between objective and subjective, public and private, political and personal).

The various forms of the writing of women's lives could be seen as inferior genres because "female"; the novel as low genre because of its readership (taking in the lower middle and working classes and importantly including women) and the commercial nature of its production for this readership, the new *public* (it was often attacked as "democratic")."The public is so stupid," commented Flaubert, whose own work marks a significant moment in the development of a split between high and low within the genre itself: on the one hand, the "literary" or "serious" novel, on the other, "popular" or "mass" fiction, the market standardization of genre products—romance, mystery, science fiction, crime, best-sellers (all the drugstore shelf-headings). The split was increasingly supported by an academic institution of literature that elaborated canons and defined quality, but the power of genre conceptions in consumer mass cultural production is indeed real. Nowhere is this more visible than in television with its host of recognized—*expected*—genres: sitcoms, news, game shows, reality shows, talk shows, et al. Such genre domination is at once part of the hierarchization process, high genres are full of *individual* works, and a fact of an entertainment industry that aims to maximize profit by organizing production around a limited number of models. Nonstandard programs, those that cross over or upset genre distinctions, can quickly become sites of disquiet and political sensitivity (witness the need felt to keep documentary and drama strictly separate, the controversies surrounding their "confusion").

This strength of genre classifications is simultaneous with a theory and practice of writing that seeks to undermine them because of their strength, the hold of ready-made expectation of meaning. "A book no longer belongs to a genre; every book answers to literature alone," asserts French writer and critic Maurice Blanchot. Or, giving up "literature" as itself another genre, the point is to shift from *work* to *text*. Where a work resembles, is readable within genre limits that it follows as a condition of its representation to the reader, the text *differs*, transgresses these limits in order to implicate the reader in a writing that disturbs representations. Where the work is on the side of pleasure, modulating a subject's cultural expectations to fulfillment, the text is on the other, that of *jouissance*, coming off from any stability of self in an abruptness of dispersal, the reader pushed out of genres. But then, inevitably, into a new one that writes the process of the subject in language; a genre that can be given a history from Mallarmé and Joyce through to the present and the texts of Blanchot himself or the deconstructive writings of Jacques Derrida, disturbingly attentive to genre laws and limits. It is this new genre that is invoked by a book such as Abdelkebir Khatibi's *L'Amour bilingue*, with its scansion of language as "bilingual," always run through by another "that asserts and destroys itself as what is incommunicable [*l'incommunicable*]." Similarly, the "writing from the body" proposed by Hélène Cixous can be understood as bound up with this same textual focus on subject and language.

These last examples point to the importance today of the need for resistances to the genre terms in a way that takes us beyond a particular French theoretical development of *le texte* as genre. Khatibi's book has "bilingualism" as a site of exploration at once in language and across languages and nations and histories and sexes: French and Arabic, France and Algeria, colonizer and colonized, man and woman, in a difficult narration of criss-crossing stories, interreacting texts. Cixous's textual practices—in novel or play or essay or dialogue—bear on the recognition and creation of a feminine writing—and those genre terms become problematic, impossible in the project of her work as it confronts generic inscriptions of gender (remember the shared etymology). A contemporary politics of genre, that is, runs askew of the lines drawn, the "legitimate" separations, discordantly mixes kinds to put literature *on the border*, the reality and metaphor of which are perhaps nowhere better exemplified than in contemporary Chicano writing with its cross-mixing border narratives (Rolando Hinojosa) and performances (Gomez-Pena) and aesthetics (*Criticism in the Borderlands* says the title of a recent work in this area).

Writing a year or so after the *fatwah* calling for the suppression of the book and its author, Salman Rushdie described the case of *The Satanic Verses* as perhaps "one of the biggest category mistakes in literary history." He was insisting on "the fictionality of fiction" and on the error of ignoring the genre of his book and reading it not as a novel but as history or antireligious pamphlet. But then the writing of *The Satanic Verses* goes contrary to an acceptance of genre orthodoxies, including those that would circumscribe the novel—"only a novel." Radically dissenting from genre segregations, its claim is for hybridity as change: "It rejoices in mongrelization and fears the absolution of the Pure. Melange, hotch-potch, a bit of this and a bit of that is *how newness enters the world*."[3] This anthology provides this claim with a section of its own, "Writing across boundaries" (precisely), but the very idea of the study *now* of *a world literature* is involved in the hybrid: reading not merely comparatively and generically, this novel from here next to that one from there, but migrationally and impurely, writings intermingled with one another, against the grain of ready—legitimate—identities. To look at genre politically is to read with just such a migrant's-eye view, which is another definition of world literature, the newness *its study makes*.

NOTES

1. Aristotle, *Poetics* [*De Poetica*] tr. Ingram Bywater: In Richard McKeon, *Introduction to Aristotle* (New York: Random House, 1947), pp. 624-667.
2. Mikhail M. Bakhtin, *The Dialogic Imagination*, ed. Michael Holquist, trans. Caryl Emerson and Michael Holquist (Austin: University Texas Press, 1981).

Christopher L. Miller

Speaking of Writing and Writing Speech: The Orality and Literacy of Literature

The idea of literature is inevitably associated with writing. The border, however, between speaking and writing in different cultures is not absolute. This essay stretches our notion of what "literacy" is as well as what is "literary" by arguing that oral traditions of expression should be considered a part of world literature.

If you have ever taken the minutes of a meeting, tried to transcribe spoken remarks from a tape recording, or attempted to recreate someone's accent in writing, you have been made aware of the gap between the spoken and the written word. Writing seems slow and cumbersome, unable to keep up with speech and capture its constantly changing inflections. In a conversation, speakers overlap, interrupt each other, and finish each other's sentences; translating that conversation into written dialogue involves hundreds of decisions. How do you deal with the hesitations, nonverbal noises ("umm," "ahem," "uh...") , and even gestures that are so much part of spoken language? Do you eliminate the contractions that are expected in speaking but not in writing? Do you construct grammatical sentences out of the oral fragments? If so, can you be sure you are not changing the meaning of what was said?

On the other hand, if you have ever read a dialogue out loud or performed in a play, you have seen how hard it is to sound "natural"—to sound as if you are speaking, not reading. It takes skill and practice to revive the energy of the oral original, or to create the illusion of doing so. If the author has not done so, you might be tempted to insert your own contractions, hesitations, and nonverbal noises. In these experiences, you are seeing the gulf between oral and written from the other side.

The complex relations between writing and speaking affect us in our daily lives. Shopping lists help us remember more than we ever could about writing; letters allow us to be clear about our thoughts and feelings. But if a friend were to come into your room and begin to read a "statement" to you about his or her feelings toward you, you might well be offended (or puzzled) by the gesture; the fact of reading itself seems to send a message of distance and formality. We expect conversations to be direct, voice-to-ear (oral/aural) encounters; writing seems to interfere with that process by introducing an extra step.

The consequences of these differences between speaking and writing have had a tremendous impact on forms of cultural expression throughout the world. The idea of literature is indissociable from writing, but the border between speaking and writing is anything but absolute.

Common sense tells us that writing is more stable than speech: writing things down not only preserves them and makes them retrievable, it also fixes their form in place, imposing rules, norms, and standards. Grammar is far more closely associated with writing than with speech. Does this mean that writing is intrinsically more disciplined and rigorous than speech, that writing imposes a superior form of thinking? Some hold this belief; but it is important to examine such claims within their historical context. In our current time and place, if writing appears to be more stable, more logical, and more reliable than speech, but if speech is livelier, more spontaneous and flexible, it does not necessarily mean that speech and writing have always been thought of in this way. In the developed countries of the Western world, competence in writing—known as literacy—is associated with education, success, and upward mobility. The term "illiteracy" is used to describe exclusion form these privileges. But in non-Western societies it is possible to see another relation between speech and writing, a relation that rests on different assumptions. For that reason we will look at some examples from Africa here, in order to gain perspective on our assumptions. Africa presents the opportunity to study both thriving oral cultures and the impact of an imposed Western literacy.

First we need to consider what writing is. Although we know what is meant by "writing" in our society (a pattern of graphic signs representing language), looking back into history shows that our system emerged from very different systems over a number of centuries and underwent significant changes over time. No one knows where or when writing was first invented. Cuneiform writing, a system of wedge-shaped signs imprinted on clay tablets, was used in Mesopotamia some six thousand years ago. Hieroglyphics appeared in Egypt between 3110 and 2884 B.C.; they represented language through standardized pictures. Hieroglyphics could be *ideograms* (representing "man" through a picture of a man) or *phonograms* (representing the sound *m* with a picture of an owl, the word for which began with that sound). Phonograms are of course closer to the phonetic alphabet that we use, which attempt to represent individual sounds rather than things themselves.

The advantages of a phonetic alphabet are obvious: with a small number of signs (such as twenty-six), thousands of words can be represented and new or unfamiliar concepts can be accommodated. With an ideographic system, thousands of individual systems must be learned one at a time. (Modern China still functions on such a system) The Roman alphabet that we use was derived from Greek, which in turn came from the Phoenician system; but the Phoenicians probably based their writing on Egyptian hieroglyphics to begin with. This means that all Western systems of writing came from Egypt. So it is interesting to consider a rumor reported by St. Augustine (*City of God,* 18.3) that it was the Ethiopians (in other words, black Africans) who first brought writing to Egypt. If true, this would mean that the African continent has a peculiar relationship with writing, as both the original source and, as we shall see, the belated receiver of Western systems whose African roots may have long since been forgotten.

What is called "writing" must therefore take a wide variety of systems into account, from ideograms to alphabets. Taking a broad view, any system of signs that represents speech or thoughts can be considered a form of writing. The "talking drums" used in certain African cultures, for example, imitate the sounds of speech and allow messages to be carried across considerable difference: is this not a kind of writing? Similarly, among the Asante people of Ghana, single brass weights in various shapes are used to represent entire proverbs. Among the Ejagham of Cameroon and Nigeria a complex system of ideographic writing was developed; it turned up in Cuba in the nineteenth century, having been brought there by enslaved Africans.[1] Systems of writing such as these must be seen as forms of literacy: in fact the world is covered with an extremely wide variety of "literacies," each with its own modes of representation.

The word "literacy" is in fact even more flexible than these examples reflect. Recently, a notion of "cultural literacy" has been invoked in the United States to describe not merely the ability to read words, but also the "mastery" of all the basic "background information" that a culture produces.[2] E.D. Hirsch, Jr., in his book *Cultural Literacy: What Every American Needs to Know,* argues that "cultural literacy lies *above* the everyday levels of knowledge that everyone possesses and *below* the expert level known only to specialists. It is that middle ground of cultural knowledge possessed by the 'common reader.' "[3] Now it is clear that in American society, Hirsch's notion of cultural literacy is indissociable from the plain ability to read and write English, from "literal" literacy. It takes a national language to sustain a national literacy; having more than one language implies more than one national-cultural literacy (as in Canada, where the use of French or English defines different cultural identities within one nation; in what used to be Yugoslavia, the choice of alphabet is a crucial sign of cultural identification between two peoples who speak the same language—the Serbs and the Croats, who speak Serbo-Croatian—but write it differently). Claiming that American literate culture—which any-one can acquire if they are given the opportunity—is "the most democratic culture in our land,"[4] Hirsch defends that culture against the claims of multiculturalism and multilingualism, which he sees as a threat; for this he has been criticized.

Leaving that controversy aside for the moment, we can take at least one lesson from Hirsch: that "cultural literacies" tend to come in units (often associated with nations) and are usually linked to a certain language. But we might well ask whether it is universally true that "cultural literacy" and "literal literacy" are inseparable. Are there cultures in which true learning is acquired and exchanged without the benefit of writing? Yes. Not only do such cultures exist, they make up the majority of the earth's civilizations, now and throughout history; furthermore, oral culture exists and thrives within all literate societies (with the possible exception of a few silent monasteries). How do cultures without writing function? What constitutes "cultural literacy" in such a society?

The term used to describe the exchange of information through speech is "orality." Anthropologists, linguists, and literary historians have strived to compare orality and literacy on a global scale. Many of their characterizations follow the common-sense patterns described above: oral societies seem more spontaneous and immediate, but with a more flexible and mythological notion of history; literate societies have a more "factual" notion of the past, but their citizens become more anonymous, as less value is attached to face-to-face encounters. Orality is thus associated with "unity" and "wholeness" but also primitivity; literacy with "progress" but also with alienation.

Looking briefly at one "oral" society will allow us to assess the validity of these characterizations. Through this example I would like to further stretch the notion of what "literacy" is by arguing that orality can be considered *a form of literacy* in the broad sense: a complex system of representation, reflecting thought and permitting the exchange of information.[5]

In the Mande society of West Africa—a culture whose permeable boundaries extend from Senegal and Guinea on the west coast through parts of Liberia and the Ivory Coast, with a heartland in western Mali—precise modes of oral exchange have organized cultural knowledge for centuries. Mande society comprises of a number of groups, including a large segment known as the "people of caste." This group is in turn composed of subgroups defined by occupation: ironsmiths, goldsmiths, leather workers, jewelers, and the bards, known as "griots." These word-smiths traditionally served as historians, messengers, matchmakers, court jesters, and advisers to kings and nobles. The griots are a separate "caste" to which one must be born; but birthright is not enough—only after extensive training can one be considered a true master of the Mande verbal arts. A master griot is then in a position to dispense and control the Mande equivalent of "cultural literacy"—through his oral recitations, listeners will acquire that "middle ground" of cultural knowledge. Griots are looked on by other segments of the society with both respect and disdain; this ambivalence stems from the attitude of Mande society toward the power of the spoken word. Speaking—and particularly the chanting of praise songs, genealogies, and epics—is traditionally considered dangerous. Speech, respected as the means of knowing who one is and where one comes from, is nonetheless distrusted because it can twist the truth into a lie; furthermore speech unleashes occult forces that can be life-threatening. Silence is considered noble, but speech is necessary for the exercise of power, so kings need griots to speak for them. When a griot performs the Mande national epic, the life story of the emperor Sunjata (who established the Mali empire in the thirteenth century), he is both defining Mande identity and earning his pay from the emperor's descendants. Griots are therefore suspected of altering the story to please the audience and increase their profit.

From this brief summary of a complex cultural question, it is possible to draw several conclusions. First, Mande orality functions according to long-established patterns that are reflected in the very structure of society; orality does not reflect a "state of nature" but rather an elaborate cultural artifice. "Cultural literacy" in the Mande requires *oral* knowledge. Furthermore, in the Mande at least, orality is not seen to be synonymous with immediacy and spontaneity: speech is already a form of representation, associated in fact with some degree of alienation (from truth, from silence, from nobility). So speech as it is understood in one African society has more in common with writing than one might think at first. It is simply wrong to associate societies "without writing" with any lack of development.

There is in fact no clear border between "literate" and "illiterate," or oral, societies. The examples of the talking drums and the Ejagham ideographs attest to this; there are forms of "writing" in all societies. In modern Western societies, much of everyday life is based on oral, not written exchange, and new technologies like television and computers have further blurred the boundaries and produced new kinds of "literacy."

In the Mande, Arabic script has been in limited use for centuries; since the nineteenth century, French-language literacy has been growing in importance, due to colonialism. The fact that a handful of European powers took over and colonized huge areas of the New World, Africa, and Asia, has everything to do with the spread of literacy as we know it. Western alphabetic writing has displaced and even supplanted oral systems and non-Western, nonalphabetic forms of writing. As they conquered, the Europeans imposed their sense of the superiority of Western alphabetic literacy. In African territories controlled by the French, the British, and the Portuguese between the late nineteenth century and 1960—virtually the entire continent—a select group of Africans was educated in colonial schools. Schooling was billed as a privilege and as the only means of access to the material well-being that the Europeans seemed to possess. The colonizers' intent was to create a new class of intermediaries between their own few, beleaguered agents and colonized masses. These go-betweens would serve as clerks, interpreters and functionaries; they would make the colonial enterprise work; to fill this role, they had to learn a European language and be able to read and write it.[6]

In the process of acquiring this literacy, Africans were often taught an ideology as well. Learning to read requires books, and colonial school "readers" contained lessons about colonialism, namely that it was beneficial to Africans. Thus a book used in French West Africa, *Les Trois Volontés de Malic* (Malic's Three Wishes, 1920), depicted a happy young Senegalese schoolboy, Malic, attending French school and preparing himself for a prosperous life. The author of the text, Ahmadou Mapaté Diagne, was Senegalese himself and a former soldier in the service of the French—he was thus part of that class of indebted, grateful intermediaries that his book sought to expand. Malic is taught that the French are the natural "friends" of all Africans and that African customs should be set aside to make way for the French, "civilized" way of doing things. Malic is inculcated with French bourgeois virtues like respect for (colonial) authority and the work ethic—virtues that will benefit the colonial order. *Malic's Three Wishes* blandly suggests that Africans abandon their own social order, and it introduces French language literacy as the first step in that process. But the most impressive part of the colonizer's message in this text is the claim that everything the French are doing in Africa will "liberate" Africans: they will be freed from ignorance, poverty, and slavery, from everything the French associate with traditional Africa (including self-governance, but that is not mentioned). All of this will come from learning to read and write French.

This text, and others like it, combined the teaching of literacy with political propaganda. Colonial literacy was something of a Trojan Horse, a gift containing an insidious threat to the African order of things.

What the colonizers did not anticipate when they started this process was that literacy could be turned against them, in a profound reversal of the colonial order. The power of literacy to establish and maintain an oppressive order was changed—by the very same class of African elite intermediaries—into a medium of protest and revolt against colonial power. those who had been trained to be obedient functionaries used their Western training to other ends: they spoke to each other (often in Paris, in French, or at Oxford, in English) and formed ideas of African authenticity, resistance, and, ultimately, independence. They developed these ideas not by abandoning the Western languages and literacies that they had been taught, but rather by exploiting them. They wrote articles, tracts, and pamphlets attacking the ideology of colonialism. But they also wrote poems, plays, and novels, thereby founding a new literature: the European-languages literature(s) of colonial and postcolonial Africa. As Benedict Anderson explains in his book *Imagined Communities*, nationalism and advanced literacy came from the same colonial milieu—namely the schools and universities.

Why did they choose this path instead of turning back to the old but not forgotten tools of orality? The simple answer is that colonialism created new cultural and political spaces—like French West Africa and British East Africa—within which no one could be effective by means of localized oral systems alone. A global problem required global means of expression, and it was clear what those were. Furthermore, in many areas, the European language was the only one with an established alphabetic writing system. If you wanted the power and advantages of literacy—the ability to influence people you have never met, across vast distances, and in the future as well—you had to use French, English, or Portuguese. Although African-language literacies are now on the rise, most writing in Africa is still done in European languages.

The seizure of the means of expression (European languages and their corresponding literacies) by colonized intellectuals is one of the most important events in twentieth-century cultural history. A comparison is often made to Shakespeare's character Caliban in *The Tempest*, a wild man on a desert island who knows no language until the wizard Prospero teaches him to speak; Caliban responds not with gratitude but with curses and the simple powerful claim: "This island's mine" (*The Tempest* I, ii). African nationalists said much the same thing.

African intellectuals thus had to work within the tension between orality and literacy. The African past was synonymous with oral traditions, which had their own structures and rules; but the new literacies had other rules that were not always compatible. Writers sought to counteract the effects of colonialism by reaching back toward the authenticity of their cultural roots; but by pursuing this project within European literacy, they were subject to its ideologies and even its censorship. How African writers were able to deal with this double bind is a complicated and fascinating question.

Djibril Tamsir Niane's *Sundiata* is a case in point. Located at the crossroads between African orality and European-language literacy (it was originally written in French), this book artfully exploits both traditions. On one level, *Sundiata* is merely the transcription of a griot's performance of the Mande national epic, as recorded and translated by Niane, who was raised in France as a historian. Thus, although the title page bears his name alone, Niane shares authorship with griot Mamadou Kouyaté whose performance the text represents. However, *Sundiata* reads much like a novel, because Niane used his skills as a writer of French to polish the text, and, presumably, to eliminate the repetitions and circumlocutions that characterize oral recitation. He also added footnotes that reflect the tension between orality and literacy. In his preface, Niane builds a new bridge between African culture and French literacy: "May this book open the eyes of more than one African and induce him to come and sit humbly beside the ancients and hear the words of the griots who teach Wisdom and History."[7] Then a new title page announces "The Words of Griot Mamadou Kouyaté," whose speech is transcribed and translated. The text thus reflects a certain *contract* between two Africans, each representing a different kind of learning, and the text is consequently a hybrid between orality and literacy.

But, halfway through the book, the contract seems to break down when Niane reports in a footnote that the griot refused to reveal secret, sacred information; the griot reaffirms the autonomy of orality against the intrusive power of literacy:

> Other people use writing to record the past, but his invention has killed the faculty of memory among them. They do not feel the past any more, for writing lacks the warmth of the human voice. With them everyone thinks he knows; but knowledge must be a secret. The prophets did not write and their words have been all the more vivid as a result. What paltry knowledge is that which is frozen inside mute books![8]

Niane nonetheless expresses a desire to "extract" all available information from the griots, in the interests of historical truth. He and Kouyaté have different notions of what is truth and what is sacred, reflecting the tension between orality and literacy. Published in 1960, the year that independence came to sixteen African states (including Senegal), *Sundiata* is symbolic of the crossroads at which African literature then found itself, suspended between old and new.

Kouyaté's critique of literacy and defense of orality did not, however, foretell any turning back of the hands of time. Since independence, most African nations have promoted European-language literacies heavily and increased literacy rates significantly. The literatures that have continued to grow in these countries have shown their ongoing ability to reverse patterns of power. Thus a novelist from the Ivory Coast named Ahmadou Kourouma became one of the first to issue a stinging attack on postcolonial governments, in his *The Suns of Independence*. The story of a Mande nobleman whose illiteracy has left him out of the post-independence boom, this novel speaks (in writing) for a strangely underprivileged group: the old nobility, left behind by the whirling modernization and westernization. But it also speaks for a group that was given little attention and no direct "voice" in literature: women. *The Suns of Independence* has one of the most memorable female characters in African fiction, Salimata, who testifies about the oppressive conditions of her life. By virtue of telling her story, Salimata begins to correct the wrongs done to her. Although a male author created her, the impact of what he wrote made him something of a feminist; and it was again within literacy that this power reversal occurred.

It is thus not surprising that African women, who had been almost completely excluded from literature until the 1970s, would, as others before them, see in literacy a means of access to power and security. One of the first Senegalese women writers, Mariama Bâ (1929-1981) included this paean to literacy in her first novel, which was concerned with a woman's coming to terms with the injustices of gender:

> The power of books, this marvelous invention of astute human intelligence, Various signs associated with sound: different sounds that form the word. Juxtaposition of words from which springs the idea, Thought, History, Science, Life. Sole instrument of interrelationships and of culture, unparalleled means of giving and receiving. Books knit generations together in the same continuing effort that leads to progress. They enabled you to better yourself.[9]

Literacy is thus indissociable from empowerment. This quotation, seen in relation to the griot Kouyaté's remarks about literacy above, says much about the changing uses of literacy in Africa. What may have been powerful once (the spoken words of the prophets, for example) does not hold the same sway in modern, postcolonial society; too much has changed. Literacy and education, not oral recitation, lead to success in modern African societies, just as they do in the West.[10]

Yet oral contact is constantly referred to and represented with literacy, as a source of "warmth" and authenticity; writing rarely detaches itself completely from a sense of "voice." Thus the narrator of So Long A Letter "speaks" directly to a friend in the text, reviving the memory of a time when their grandmothers "exchanged messages" across the fence between their yards.[11] Thus political power is often known as "having a voice." Literature constantly draws its sustenance and its claim to realism from the representation of speech. In American literature, Mark Twain, Flannery O'Connor, and Alice Walker (among countless others) have all lent a sense of specific milieu to their characters by imitating dialect in writing.

Orality and literacy must therefore be seen within the complexities of their constantly shifting alliance. There is no "orality" without "writing"—without some degree of representation; there are only degrees of representation, various degrees of removal from thought itself. Nor is there a literacy that is not in some way derived from or influenced by the power of speech. In any time and place, there are important differences between orality and literacy, but we must not leap to conclusions about those differences. What we call literature is indebted to both.

NOTES

1. See Robert Farris Thompson, *The Flash of the Spirit* (New York: Random House, 1983).

2. E.D. Hirsch, Jr., *Cultural Literacy: What Every American Needs to Know* (New York: Random House, 1987), pp. 2 and 18.

3. Ibid., p. 19.

4. Ibid., p. 21.

5. On this point, see also Jacques Derrida, "The Violence of the Letter: From Lévi-Strauss to Rousseau" in *Of Grammatology*, trans. Gayatri Chakravorty Spivak (Baltimore and London: Johns Hopkins University Press, 1974), pp. 101-140.

6. See Benedict Anderson, *Imagined Communities: Reflections on the Origin and Spread of Nationalism* (London and New York: Verso, 1983).

7. Djibril Tamsir Niane, *Sundiata: An Epic of Old Mali*. Essex: Longman, 1986. (1960), p.viii.

8. Ibid., pp. 40-41.

9. Miriama Bâ, *So Long a Letter* (London: Heinemann, 1981), p. 32.

10. For an analysis of similar patterns in African-American culture, see Vera Kutzinski, ch. 2 "The Black Limbo" in *Against the American Grain* (Baltimore: Johns Hopkins University Press, 1987), pp. 47-130; see also Gayl Jones, *Liberating Voices: Oral Traditions in African-American Literature* (Cambridge, Mass.: Harvard University Press, 1991).

11. Bâ, p. 1.

A conversation-collage based on writings by
Susan Gubar, Carolyn G. Heilbrun,
bell hooks [Gloria Watkins], Myra Jehlen and
Catharine R. Stimpson.

Gender Reading

The term "gender" in literary criticism refers not only to women but more broadly to the way we structure our understanding of literature through the lens of gender. Certain works or styles when described as "feminine" or "manly" reveal our cultural assumptions about sexual identity that then affect our critical perceptions and vocabularies. We have to invent ourselves through our texts.

We have wanted to present several voices on this issue, and so have tried to weave together a few strands concerning the complexities of gender and women's lives, of race and class, of binary systems and of moral/textual practice.

Myra Jehlen's article on "Gender" in *Critical Terms for Literary Study* sets the discussion in general terms, when she ponders exactly what happens if a character like Hamlet, say, is "taken as embodying the general human condition. Ironically such transcendent characterization works reductively to submerge the complexities of human difference," she says, pointing out the existence of differences between men and women that ought not to be subsumed under the term, "general human condition." Can we assume that Hamlet sees the world from the point of view of Ophelia?

A critic, Jehlen continues, "needs to focus precisely on the distinctions, qualifications and complexities of human difference," situating people in their own time, place, gender, race, and class. For what is at stake is what we mean by the terms, "human," "feminine," and "manly," in our daily use. In acknowledging that our meanings are humanly created and reflect the historical and cultural needs and pressures of the moment, we adopt a critical stance toward gender that works against the "fantasy of transcendence." We speak not of the "human condition," but of the condition of men and women in different times and places in cultural flux. This criticism "conscious of literature's and its own sexual politics affirms the permanent complexity" of human relations, amid the changing engagements and interactions.

This should suggest what it is useful nonetheless to say explicitly: that speaking of gender does not mean speaking only of women. As a critical term "gender" invokes women only insofar as in its absence they are essentially invisible. And it brings them up not only for their own interest but to signal the sexed nature of men as well, and beyond that the way the sexed nature of both women and men is not natural but cultural. In this sense, gender may be opposed to sex as culture is to nature so that its relation to sexual nature is unknown and probably unknowable: how, after all, do we speak of human beings outside of culture? From the perspective of gender, identity is a role, character traits are not autonomous qualities but functions and ways of relating. Actions define actors rather than vice versa. Connoting history and not nature, gender is not a category of human nature.

Uncovering the contingencies of gender at the heart of even the most apparently universal writing has been a way of challenging the view that men embody the transcendent human norm, a view to which the first objection was that it was unjust to women. But in proposing gender as a basic problem and an essential category in cultural and historical analysis, feminists have recast the issue of women's relative identity as equally an issue for men, who, upon ceasing to be mankind, become, precisely, men. Thus gender has emerged as a problem that is always implicit in any work. It is a quality of the literary voice hitherto masked by the static of common assumptions. And as a critical category gender is an additional lens, or a way of lifting the curtain to an unseen recess of the self and of society. Simply put, the perspective of gender enhances the critical senses....

This perspective serves as a moral-aesthetic intensification of our reading sensitivities, and our writing of new views and plots appropriate to them.

Though speaking of gender does not mean speaking only of women, this is a time when many critics are rereading literature and creating new stories about women. Susan Gubar describes ways in which women are engaged in creating parables "in an ongoing revisioning of female theology." As part of this revision, she discusses Isak Dinesen's story "The Blank Page," one of many several-pronged parables that are being reinterpreted:

> Briefly, the story of "The Blank Page" centers on the sisters of a Carmelite order of nuns who grow flax to manufacture the most exquisite linen in Portugal. This linen is so fine that it is used for the bridal sheets of all the neighboring royal houses. After the wedding night, it is solemnly and publicly displayed to attest to the virginity of the princess and is then reclaimed by the convent, there the central piece of the stained sheet "which bore witness to the honor of a royal bride" is mounted, framed, and hung in a long gallery with a plate identifying the name of the princess. These "faded markings" on the sheets are of special interest to female pilgrims who journey to the remote country convent, for "each separate canvas with its coroneted name-plate has a story to tell, and each has been set up in loyalty to the story." But pilgrims and sisters alike are especially fascinated by the framed canvas over the one nameless plate which displays the blank, snow-white sheet that gives the story its title.
>
> Before approaching the mysterious promise of this blank page, let us consider the framed, bloodied sheets in the convent gallery, which is both a museum of women's paintings (each sheet displays a unique, abstract design and is mounted in a heavy frame) and a library of women's literary works (the bloodstains are ink on these woven sheets of paper). Collected and cherished by a female community that has seen better days, a kind of paradigmatic women's studies department, these bloodstained marks illustrate at least two points about female anatomy and creativity: first, many women experience their own bodies as the only available medium for their art, with the result that the distance between the woman artist and her art is often radically diminished; second, one of the most primary and most resonant metaphors provided by the female body is blood,

and cultural forms of creativity are often experienced as a painful wounding.[2]

The wound at the heart of the feminist text remains vivid, lending not only its potential tragedy—and the difficult triumph over that initial marking, often by means of anger—but more positively, its excessive and provocative color to the ongoing, collective work of the feminist community. The Dinesen story, included in the *World Reader*, illustrates the spirit and body of this community as it reads, remembers, and preserves, the pages stained and blank as sheets, where the text is both gravely embodied and dramatically empowering to the reader next-to-come. What is the body of this text? Its body is, literally, its meaning.

"The Blank Page" also implies that female creativity—the "framed sheets" of the wedding night or of women's literary works—is often nurtured in the body of a female community. So bell hooks tells the story of her grandmother who spent a lifetime making quilts among women, and this became central to her self-expression as the family historian:

> Baba spent a lifetime making quilts, and the vast majority of her early works were crazy quilts. When I was a young girl she did not work outside her home, even though she at one time worked for white people, cleaning their houses. For much of her life as a rural black woman she controlled her own time, and quilting was part of her daily work. Her quilts were made from reused scraps because she had access to such material from the items given her by white folks in place of wages, or from the worn clothes of her children. It was only when her children were adults faring better economically that she began to make quilts from patterns and from fabric that was not reused scraps. Before then she created patterns from her imagination. My mother, Rosa Bell, remembers writing away for the first quilt patterns. The place these quilts had in daily life was decorative. Utility quilts, crazy quilts were for constant everyday use. They served as bed coverings and as padding under the soft cotton mattresses filled with feathers. During times of financial hardship which were prolonged and ongoing, quilts were made from scraps left over from dressmaking and then again after the dresses had been worn. Baba would show a quilt and point to the same fabric in a lighter color to show a "fresh" scrap (one left over from initial

dressmaking) from one that was being reused after a dress was no longer wearable.

When her sons went away to fight in wars, they sent their mother money to add rooms to her house. It is a testament to the seriousness of Baba's quiltmaking that one of the first rooms she added was a workplace, a space for sewing and quiltmaking. I have vivid memories of this room because it was so unusual. It was filled with baskets and sacks full of scraps, hatboxes, material pieced together that was lying on the backs of chairs. There was never really any place to sit in that room unless one first removed fabric. This workplace was constructed like any artist's studio, yet it would not be until I was a young woman and Baba was dead that I would enter a "real" artist's studio and see the connection. Before this workplace was built, quilting frames were set up in the spacious living room in front of the fire. In her workplace quilts were stored in chests and under mattresses. Quilts that were not for use, fancy quilts (which were placed at the foot of beds when company came) were stored in old-fashioned chests with beautiful twisted pieces of tobacco leaves that were used to keep insects away. Baba lived all her life in Kentucky—tobacco country. It was there and accessible. It had many uses.

Although she did not make story quilts, Baba believed that each quilt had its own narrative—a story that began from the moment she considered making a particular quilt. The story was rooted in the quilt's history, why it was made, why a particular pattern was chosen. In her collection there were the few quilts made for bringing into marriage. Baba talked often of making quilts as preparation for married life. After marriage most of her quilts were utility quilts, necessary bed covering. It was later in life, and in the age of modernity, that she focused on making quilts for creative pleasure. Initially she made fancy quilts by memorizing patterns seen in the houses of the white people she worked for. Later she bought patterns. Working through generations, her quiltmaking reflected both changes in the economic circumstances of rural black people and changes in the textile industry. . . .

To share the story of a given quilt was central to Baba's creative self-expression, as family historian, storyteller, exhibiting the work of her hands. She was not particularly fond of crazy quilts because they were a reflection of work motivated by material necessity. She liked organized design and fancy quilts. They expressed a quiltmaker's seriousness. her patterned quilts, "the Star of David," "The Tree of Life," were made for decorative purposes, to be displayed at family reunions. They indicated that quiltmaking was an expression of skill and artistry. These quilts were not to be used; they were to be admired. My favorite quilts were those for everyday use. I was especially fond of the work associated with my mother's girlhood. When given a choice of quilts I selected one made of cotton dresses in cool deep pastels. Baba could not understand when I chose that pieced fabric of little stars made from my mother's and sister's cotton dresses over more fancy quilts. Yet those bits and pieces of mama's life, held and contained there, remain precious to me.[3]

The whole point is what we can *make precious*, holding it up and out as such, and what we can preserve. It is the space of feminism that permits the community of writing women to make meaning of their lives, with the sustaining "sense of group purpose" of which Catharine R. Stimpson speaks in her introduction to *Where the Meanings Are*, presenting this space and this purpose as what is most worth finding:

So questing, so questioning, I have found feminism a space where meanings are. Here, Emily Dickinson, Virginia Woolf, and other women of language become richer, deeper, at once more enigmatic and more clear. Some naive notions of intergalactic space have described it as empty, blank, a cleaned-out vacuum. However, sharper scrutinies see forms and matter in the void. Similarly, some naive notions for our intra-global cultures project women as silent beings. If they speak, they babble. However, feminism provides a hearing room and a reading room in which to realize how energetic women's engagements with language have been; how inventively women have strung language along.

• • •

Primarily, feminism responds to sex and gender differences in which those differences signify, justify, and ratify one sex's domination of the other: male over female, men over women, masculine values over feminine. No feminist likes domination: rote, rotten, and brute authority. For a feminist, space is a location in which to roam, play, plant, and settle: not in which to bluster and bully, or, in response, to cower and huddle.

• • •

In law, the argument about sexual difference has appeared in struggles about "protective legislation." In arts and letters, it emerges when critics think about the possibility of a "female language" or "female brush-stroke" or "female eye" or "female sense of space." A minimalist, like me, will suggest that it means something that Virginia Woolf, as she dashed off a letter, was a woman. However, exactly what it means depends on her time, place, languages, and circumstance. On the other hand, a maximalist might read in Woolf's syntax, rhythms, and alphabets a "femaleness," a nature, that unifies women in all their times, places, languages, and circumstance.

Sophisticated though the arguments about sex and gender difference can be, they edge towards an error in which failures of logic, perception, and behavior can compound together. This error is clinging to binary oppositions. At their most benign, binary oppositions over-simplify categorizing as the missionary position does sex. At their most malign, translated into an active belief in "Good Us, Bad Them, Praise Us, Get Them," binary oppositions damage the interests of survival itself.[4]

A refusal of the too-simple binary divisions the world is often set up in or by, while it entails a rejection of categories too tightly defined, permits an "exercise in feminist intertextualities," and a "process of reading through rather than towards."[5]

Most important of all, these bits and pieces of our lives and our grandmother's lives, as in Baba's quilt, all these pages blank and marked with our wounds and our past, all our desires for making a new life and a new story—in the terms of our new individual and collective questions and questings, heroic and ordinary—respond to each other in the texts we live by and through. World literature, as we now read it, with its myths and its reality, its gods and persons and characters not unlike our own, has to be infused with the same questing spirit in which the new feminist criticism so clearly abounds.

This conversation-collage is really about having the courage to read our texts or those of others, to tell our stories *differently*. Carolyn Heilbrun insists on how we have to aim toward that quest that has kept returning the length of this collective essay, how we have not to let our plots be told for us. We must now, we do now, re-read and re-fable narratives from the Greeks to the present:

> Within the quest plot, men might do anything: literature tells us all they have done. Within the marriage plot women might only wait to be desired, to be wed, to be forgotten: as Tennyson more or less puts it, to be perhaps, after the first passion is over, nearer to a man than his horse and dog, but not much nearer. The question women must all ask is how to be freed from the marriage plot and initiated into the quest plot. How many women today find a script, a narrative, a story to live by?
>
> It is, of course, ironic that Freud's annoying question of what do women want must still haunt us. It is not a question we can answer, because we cannot tell stories we have never heard. We women today who have entered the public sphere exist there in a state of intermittent anxiety and pain. Nor is it possible to foretell the source of the pain or the pattern it will follow. When women have had their stories written for them, played out their destinies toward marriage or death, they knew the pain that might follow: the first penetration; childbirth; rejection; aging; the suffering of one's children; the diverted attention of one's husband; the rending away from women whose place, like one's own, changed at the behest of male relatives. Pain in not easier for having been suffered before in the same way, but it is more bearable for having been narrated. That, indeed, is the chief source of patriarchal power: that it is embodied in unquestioned narratives. But for women today in new places and new jobs, there is no story to explain the pain, which is as unexpected as it is acute. We have been told, if we were kind and loving, we would be loved in return. In the public sphere, this is not true, and it must be learned on the pulses. Even when we have grown tough and knowledgeable, the power of phallocracy is appalling. We invent as we go along, support one another, and recognize, as we must, that our choice is, as Florence Nightingale long ago told us, between pain and paralysis.

One cannot make up stories: one can only retell in new ways the stories one has already heard. Let us agree on this: that we live our lives through texts. These may be read, or chanted, or experienced electronically, or come to us, like the murmurings of our mothers, telling us of what conventions demand. Whatever their form or medium, these stories are what have formed us all, they are what we must use to make our new fictions. Since it is these stories—let me call them tales as a general term encompassing everything from Greek myths through Genesis, Snow White, General Hospital, and pac man—from which we shall form the new fictions of our lives, we must ask what tales seem to be available to us today out of which to make women's fictions that are not based upon Derrida's male/female opposition, where male is always dominant. We cannot yet make wholly new fictions; we can only transform old tales, and recognize how women have transformed old tales in the past. Out of old tales, we must make new lives.

What exactly do I mean when I say that we must make up new lives and new fictions? It becomes important, I think, to distinguish carefully between "fiction" and "myth." Not "myth" as in the stories of the Greek gods and heroes, but "myth" in the sense of the sustaining narratives of an ideology. Myth, Frank Kermode tells us, "operates within the diagrams of ritual, which presupposes total and adequate explanations of things as they are, and were: it is a sequence of radically unchangeable gestures." Myths are agents of stability and call for absolute assent. Fictions, on the other hand, "are for finding things out, and they change as the needs of sense-making change." An English writer, Angela Carter, has put it another way: "Myth deals in false universals, to dull the pain of particular circumstances." A fair definition of myth is consolatory nonsense. It tells us how society says we must live, rather than teaching us how we might learn to live.

You will understand, then, what I mean when I say women must make new fictions of their lives, forsaking the myths they have for millenniums been taught.

What I like best to remember, however, was Samuel Butler's inclusion among his arguments, most of them misogynistic, for

why the *Odyssey* had been written by a woman. "When Ulysses
and Penelope are in bed," he wrote, "and are telling their stories
to one another, Penelope tells hers first. I believe a male writer
would have made Ulysses' story come first, and Penelope's
second." But of course, we know the answer is not that the
Odyssey was written by a woman, but that we have already heard
Odysseus' story, between Books 4 and 16. We know it, it is one
of the narratives on which we have been nurtured. But
Penelope's is a new story, a story of a woman's choice, her
anxiety and her terror, and it must be heard now by the man
who, despite all temptations, returned to her, and to the decisions he could trust her to make. He who had traveled far and
seen many marvelous things, listened first to the new story of
the woman who, staying home, had traveled to a new place of
experience, had created a new narrative, who had been able,
finally, to stop unweaving and to invent a new story.[6]

NOTES

1. Myra Jehlen, "Gender" in *Critical Terms for Literary Study*, ed. Frank
    Lentricchia and Thomas McLaughlin (Chicago and London: University of
    Chicago Press,), p. 265.
2. Susan Gubar, "The Blank Page and Female Creativity," in *Writing and Sexual
    Difference*, ed. Elizabeth Abel (Chicago: University of Chicago Press, 1982),
    pp. 77-78.
3. bell hooks, *Yearning: Race, Gender and Cultural Politics* (Boston: South End
    Press, 1990), pp. 119-121.
4. Catharine R. Stimpson, *Where the Meanings Are: Feminism and Cultural Spaces*
    (London and New York: Methuen, 1988), p. 94.
5. Nancy K. Miller, *Getting Personal* (New York: Routledge, 1991), p. 75.
6. Carolyn Heilbrun, *Hamlet's Mother and Other Essays* (New York: Ballantine,
    1990), pp. 127-30.

Shirley Geok-lin Lim

Place, Exile, and A-filiation: Migrant and Global Literatures

More literature is now being written by authors who have voluntarily or involuntarily separated from their places of birth. This position of "exile" leads many writers to question traditional notions of identity, home and nation. In so doing, they have begun to create "global" literature, different from the tradition of nationally-bounded literatures.

Critical awareness of the cooperation or the absence of cooperation between birthplace and identity can be crucially missing in literary canons that categorize by national distinctions. For example, in the United States the popular representation of the immigrant's successful assimilation tends to elide the history and present of other immigrants—the illegals, refugees, poor and working class—who are recast as "others." The immigrant success story reproduces the epic of the United States as the nation of limitless opportunity, freedom, and triumphant individualism. The master narrative of individual autonomy, economic competition, and race-assimilation often masks the convergence of the discourse of nationalism with that of race.[1]

The convergence of race with national identity is demonstrated in contemporary global politics that continue to cast immigrants as a race problem. According to the United Nations Population Fund, about 70 million people now work legally or illegally in countries of which they are not native-born citizens. Their numbers grow annually, as two million refugees and immigrants are added to them. While the United States is a primary destination for immigrants from Asia and Central America, high birthrates in North Africa and other parts of the developing world also lead to immigration pressures on Europe.[2] The French newspaper *Le Figaro* estimates that one-quarter of the total population of France is of "foreign origin."[3] Although these immigrants are needed to work in jobs that nationals no longer desire, they are perceived as "strangers" and "aliens."

This geo-political phenomenon has cultural consequences, for, as people move from their natal territories, notions of individual and group identity grounded in ideas of geographical location as a national homeland and of segregated racial purity are contested, and weaken. Although original inhabitants "increasingly feel they are under cultural and economic siege," Europe, like the United States, may be destined "to become multicultural societies."[4] The literatures being produced today by immigrant populations *and* by nationalists reflect, express, address, and reconstruct the late twentieth-century preoccupation with and interrogation of concepts of identity, home, and nation, whether through recuperating ideals of tribal origin and community, through reinscribing the modern invention of nationalism as a political strategy for social organization, or through negotiating the unstable territory of the minority subject or destabilized psyche through a cosmopolitan elite attached to an ideology of the autonomous subject. Nicolás Guillén's poem "My Last Name," for example, questions the Spanish ancestry provided by his Cuban Hispanic name and claims an "ancestral blood" that is "Mandingo, Bantu, Yoruba, Dahoman." In recovering African "roots of my roots," the poem also mocks and rejects the ties of acknowledged patrimony in order to celebrate the foreign:

> Good friends, what does it matter?
> ....
> My name without end,
> made up of endless names;
> my name, foreign,
> free and mine, foreign and yours,
> foreign and free as the air.

The debate surrounding a writer's identity and national boundary identity, moreover, is not simply one of admitting immigrant voices into a national canon or even of favoring a multicultural over a monocultural society. We see today the emergence of a global culture on a scale where events taking place in once remote places of the earth are acknowledged as directly affecting distant peoples. The ecology movement teaches us that actions taken by different groups of people, from the Amazonian Indians to the automobile industry workers in Detroit, affect all groups. That is one example of the dynamics of a global culture. That the ecologists' message can now be transmitted simultaneously through mass media to the peoples of the world is another.

This global culture must be distinguished from the globalization of cultures, the changes within separate societies in response to increasingly transnational forces, such as the multinational and corporate nature of the publishing industry or of most late-capitalist industries. Even without the movements of refugees and immigrants that break down the historically recent constructions of social identity around the nation-state, the new technologies of travel, media, and industry both subvert these constructions and lead to renewed state efforts to control and patrol their physical and cultural borders. These technologies, increasing in global reach and effect, relate and commingle cultures once separated by tribal, racial, and national distinctiveness, which are thus less able to protect themselves from uncontrolled change or unwanted influence from alien cultures.

The literature produced by "metropolitan" writers across boundaries is thus open to contradictory interpretations. One reading situates the writing as interrupting or challenging the authority of metropolitan culture; as, for example, in Louise Bennett's poem "Colonization in Reverse." Another reading interprets the popular publication and reception of texts produced by writers who are situated outside their natal borders—especially those works that can be taken to illustrate Western notions of Asian corruption, or Western practices of postmodernism—as entailing a weakening of their strangeness, and finally incorporation of the alien. The transformation of the non-natal through interpretative affiliations may lead to a case like Naipaul's *The Enigma of Arrival* being seen as a "British" text, although the actual practice of his writing makes that incorporation problematic.

The binarism of place (filiation) and identity (affiliation) which gives rise to national canonical categories, even though inclusive of immigrant contributions, needs to be re-thought to admit two other categories, exile (exfiliation) and a-filiation. I define exfiliation or exilic experience as the condition of being outside the natal order, a condition specified in space and time, always conditioned by place and history, and characterized by the keen anguish of events that have a beginning and a hope of an end. Literatures of exile have become increasingly evident as wars, famines, and natural disasters result in larger and larger involuntary dislocations of entire groups of people, from the European Jews displaced during the Second World War (see Isaac Bashevis Singer's "The Cafeteria") to Filipinos living in the United States (see San Juan's "Voyages"). Nabokov's witty poem "An Evening of Russian Poetry," for example, weaves together two languages, English and Russian. English is the language of instruction: in the mouths of the interlocutors, a banal discourse; and in the poet's voice, a combination of colloquial patter, social humor, and profound wit. Russian, as the object of inquiry, is the translated language, the language of the speaker's affections, whose betrayal for cash and for another tongue leads to the self-reflexive irony that permeates the poem. Significantly, therefore, the most emotional lines, concluding the poem, are spoken first in Russian, the beloved language of the heart, then translated into English. The different attitudes toward English (the place/language of exile) and Russian (the place/language of home) in the poem intersect poignantly to suggest the exile's uneasy sense of betrayal of origin.

I distinguish the category of a-filiation as an imagined condition of being without, without the desire and anguish that distinguish the exilic imagination, without family, without the affiliation of institutions and nation, demonstrating provisionality and exigency in their most immediate form. To this category, I would assign the literature of the transnational, the "minority" status of a Kafka, for example, described by Deleuze and Guattari in terms of a "deterritorialization" of language and imagination exhibited in works attending "the decomposition and fall of the Empire," when a work turns away from the dream of filling "a major language function" and uses its polylingualism instead to "find its point of non-culture and underdevelopment."[5] Many works written from the position of the ex-colonial or postcolonial—for example, Frantz Fanon's *Black Face, White Mask*—attempt acts of deterritorialization and reterritorialization, locating themselves through their critiques of both "native" and "colonial" historical and cultural domination from a position of a-filiation.

More and more literature is being produced from the subject position of exile, the condition of voluntary or involuntary separation from one's place of birth, and of a-filiation. Alootook Ipellie's poem "Walking Both Sides of an Invisible Border," directly addresses the paradoxical condition of living without defined and protective national boundaries while attempting to balance disparate cultural worlds:

> Walking in two different worlds
> Trying my best to make sense
> Of two opposing cultures
> Which are unable to integrate
> Lest they swallow one another whole.

Vladimir Nabokov and Czeslaw Milosz, although from very different backgrounds, are writers whose works can be seen in the context of the twentieth-century phenomenon of postcolonial and post-World War social and refugee movements. Both European emigrés, they write through a wide spectrum of a-filiative positions that can be read either in a European or an American context. The poetry of Derek Walcott demonstrates a shift from an original home in his Saint Lucia culture to an a-filiative position that appropriates Africa, Europe, and the Americas for literary allusions. Works by V.S. Naipaul and Salman Rushdie, similarly, no longer comply with the usual forms of immigrant/national literatures. As literatures of migratory exile, produced within an Anglophone global culture, their works challenge the mythic narratives of homeland, question the disquiet of nostalgia (translated as homesickness in the original Greek form), and reveal identity as historically created in a manner that also interrogates the given identities of their patron societies.

Both global traditions, read together, illustrate a recent multifaceted cultural phenomenon, produced within the borders of the metropolitan state by migrant and diasporic intellectuals, a phenomenon different in kind from immigrant writing. However, many reviewers of such works insist on their "national" or "metropolitan" qualities. In this collapse of the diasporic intellectual into the amnesiac condition of the "metropolitan," one with no life history before arrival at the metropolitan culture, these commentators repeat orthodox myths regarding immigrant absorption. Indeed, some metropolitan fiction, such as that written by Mukherjee, beginning from an exilic position, is concerned with affiliative cooperation, with finding a place within the idea of the welcoming New World.

Benedict Anderson, in his study of nationalism, points to the emergence of print-capitalism or print-language as providing the basis for national consciousness.[6] However, as publishing becomes absorbed into the circulation of late-twentieth-century international corporate capital, it now arguably lays the groundwork for a transnational consciousness that undermines national consciousness. Much diaspora literature has become a highly marketable product: thus one can read in the privileging of diasporic works by Derek Walcott, V.S. Naipaul, Salman Rushdie or Czeslaw Milosz the convergence of capitalism and print technology to create the possibility of a new form of "imagined community," but a community/nation that is Western metropolitan rather than non-Western national.

Moreover, it is not only the choice of the English language and of Western publishers that has consequences for the community that the texts are seen to refer to. The context of diplomatic history in which the interpretive community is situated also affects the community constructed in the text and the kinds of community addressed by the text. In contemporary geopolitics, the West is identified with international corporate capital. The slippery subject of diasporic literature is often taken by writers and their audience to suggest that assimilation into this corporate world is innocent, natural, inevitable, and valuable. In the progression from natal origin to metropolitan inhabitant represented in much a-filiative writing, home is constructed as always absent, as never having really existed. The void of origin prepares the reader for the construction of the metropolis as material vitality, and for the resolution in favor of an international culture based on capital. The loss of place and the removal of exilic themes consequent upon this loss replaces an a-filiative sensibility in terms of which the individual psyche is attached to a social world now without traditional place or national boundaries. Jorge Luis Borges's poem "The Web," pondering the unstable exigencies of history that ironically produce our seemingly stable constructs of identity, concludes that central questions of place and language

> form part of the fateful web
> of cause and effect
> that no man can foresee,
> nor any god.

But there is another tradition of writing by transnationals of multiple diasporas that resists this interpretation. Han Suyin's four-volume autobiography and Edward Said's critical work are prime examples of such a tradition, in which the West is one agent in a diplomatic relationship with China or Palestine. This position opens up questions of affiliation that suggest a different history of the individual imagination as moving between at least two cultural systems, each undermining and reconfiguring the other as a kind of "intranationalism." Such works, constructing a contestory relation between place and identity, compose a tradition of "global literature" different from the tradition of nationally bounded and divided identities that has conventionally organized our understanding of "world literature."

NOTES

1. Etienne Balibar and Immanuel Wallerstein, *Race, Nation, Class: Ambiguous Identities* (London: Verso, 1991) p. 37.

2. Stanley Meisler, "Rising Wind of Migration," *Los Angeles Times*, Apr. 30, 1992; p. A9.

3. René Tempest, "France Is the Immigration Litmus Test," *Los Angeles Times*, Oct. 1, 1991; p. M8.

4. Judith Miller, "Strangers at the Gate," *New York Times Magazine*, Sept. 15, 1991; pp. 32 and 37.

5. Gilles Deleuze and Felix Guattari, "What Is a Minor Literature?" *Mississippi Review* 11 (3): 25.

6. Benedict Anderson, *Imagined Communities: Reflections of the Origin and Spread of Nationalism* (London: Verso, 1983), p. 46.

Mary Beard

Culturally Variable Ways of Seeing: Art and Literature

It is important to remind ourselves that our own systems of belief influence the way we understand and interpret world literature. This essay brings into the open our "rules for looking." Such rules exist—though we may not always be aware of them—and they are culturally variable, differing from culture to culture.

We tend to take the process of *looking* very much for granted; and we rarely stop to reflect on how we make sense of what we see. It is a striking contrast with our engagement in the process of *reading*. Not only do most of us still remember the struggles of first learning to read, the difficulties of decoding those baffling symbols on the page, but even as well-practiced, adult readers we constantly remind ourselves of the problems of understanding and interpreting texts: when was this text written? Does its age affect our understanding? Who was it written for? Why? What language was it first written in? What difference does the translation make? So, for example, we would hardly try to read the Psalms, the Acts of Buddha, or the Koran without recollecting that these are religious texts, part of a system of beliefs that we perhaps do not share. Nor would we seriously try to read early Chinese love poetry, or attempt to understand the passions of Racine's *Phaedra* or Shakespeare's Prospero without any thought for their historical context: however immediate, even modern, the emotions expressed might at first seem, our reading is almost inevitably affected by the knowledge that "being in love" in ancient China or Elizabethan England may have been quite a different experience (governed by quite different rules and constraints) from "being in love" in the contemporary West.

Compare the very casual approach we take to looking. We are often happy to look without thinking, and to allow ourselves to enjoy images as "pure," with little regard for their context, history, or cultural difference. We may admire, for example, the glittering icons of Byzantium without reflecting on their original purpose as devotional, religious images, just as we often enjoy the luxuriant miniatures of ladies at the Indian court without considering the social and economic circumstances that produced such images. Of course, we are not always so casual. Some images do remain for us firmly rooted in their historical context, or in the ideology that created them. If someone, for example, chose reproductions of Nazi art as home decoration, even now that would be a strident political statement; we would hardly believe any claim that it was just an aesthetic admiration for the paintings. Similarly with Picasso's *Guernica:* few viewers consider the painting without at the same time reflecting on the atrocities of the Spanish Civil War that were its inspiration. But all the same, a glance at most dormitory walls (with their wild juxtapositions of images—postcards of Botticelli next to Salvador Dali, native American textiles next to Hokusai waves) suggests that in the visual field "anything goes."

This atmosphere of free play can be liberating. It allows us to use the images *for ourselves*, without becoming lost in the intricacies of historical context or original purpose; it allows us to fix the images freely into our own personal stories ("this postcard is a souvenir of the time when I...." or "This poster reminds me of..."). But at the same time the casualness tends to conceal from us the processes which lie behind the ways we make sense of, judge, and rank the images we see. It encourages us not to examine our *rules for looking*. These are the rules that govern things as basic as our classification of artistic production ("major art," "minor arts," "art," "artefact," "craft," "Western art," "tribal art," and so on), the language we use to discuss this production, and the value we choose to give it.

The aim of this essay is to bring out into the open some of these rules for looking. It tries to show not only that such rules do exist, however concealed they may be in everyday life, but also that—as the title suggests—they are *culturally variable;* that is, they are not universal but differ from one culture or cultural subgroup to another. It follows from this variability that the rules themselves may be a source of disagreement or conflict within any society—but particularly within the diffuse amalgam of cultures that makes up modern North America and many other modern-nation states. This essay examines some of the cases where such conflict has become open, even fierce; and it tries to show that these instances of explicit disagreement about our "ways of seeing" are not just peculiar exceptions, but can help us more generally to uncover the rules that underlie our practice of viewing—rules that normally remain concealed, implicit, and unexamined.

The focus of what follows is the museum and art gallery. It is not, of course, the case that art exists only within those institutions. There are all kinds of visual images in private houses, in churches, in dormitories, in hospitals. But nevertheless, over the last two hundred years the museum has become the privileged location for art; the museum is the place we now look to as the guardian of art, the place whose rules play a large part in defining our ways of seeing. As is obvious, the vast majority of the pictures in this book illustrate objects or paintings that (whatever their original location) are now housed in museums.

In the mid 1980s a large exhibition of Hispanic art was shown in various galleries across the United States. It gathered together probably the most comprehensive collection of contemporary paintings and sculptures produced by American artists of Hispanic descent ever to be shown in major national museums. The exhibition's organizers had set out to bring before a wider American public the work of artists normally neglected by mainstream art institutions, and to assert the importance of Hispanic art as part of contemporary American culture. They almost certainly did not foresee the intense controversies that the exhibition would arouse.

The terms of the conflict were very clear. On the one hand there were the well-intentioned, liberal aims of the organizers who saw themselves as expanding the range of the traditional art museum, widening the horizons of the American museum-going public, and at the same time doing justice to Hispanic artists by granting them their rightful place in great national institutions. On the other hand there were those who objected to the cultural imperialism of the mainstream galleries, which (as they saw it) were attempting to take over, domesticate, and so depoliticize Chicano artistic productions. To turn Hispanic art into "Art," to pull murals off street walls and place them as "museum objects" in the institutions of the dominant culture was, so the argument went, to undermine the whole significance of the Hispanic art movement. The rightful place of Hispanic art, in other words, was on the streets, not in the museum.

This debate is part of an irresolvable series of questions about the place of Hispanic art and about how we should look at it. Should Hispanic art always exist on the margins of the dominant artistic culture? How can that dominant culture recognize the work of Hispanic artists without merely appropriating them? Why would Chicano artists *want* to show their work in the Metropolitan Museum? Or why, on the other hand, should they be content never to be shown there? Why should "we" not be free to display and view Hispanic art wherever and however we want? Who has the right to decide where this art belongs? But underlying these questions, even wider issues come into play: namely, the fact that the context in which we view art *matters;* that a painting hung on a museum wall necessarily means something different from the same painting displayed in the street; that we process and understand images in one way when we view them in the calm, quiet, reverent atmosphere of the art museum and in quite other ways when we see them at the back of the parking lot.

It is easy enough to recognize these various options and differences when we are thinking of contemporary art, within the society with which we are most familiar. So even if we do not wholeheartedly agree with the complaints of some of the Chicano artists, we can readily understand what is at stake in their objections. It is rather more difficult to see the force of such issues immediately when we are viewing art that was produced at much greater distance from us—centuries old, perhaps, or from an unfamiliar foreign culture. But here, too, conflict, choices, and options in viewing lie just beneath the surface. How can we recapture them for ourselves?

Imagine that you are in an art museum looking at a painting by an artist of the Italian Renaissance; let's suppose it is *The Baptism of Christ* by Piero della Francesca (1416?-1492). How does the museum encourage you to see and understand this picture? What story does it try to construct around it? Maybe the label beside the painting is very brief, telling you only the name of the artist, the title, and date of the world of art; maybe there is not much explicit guidance about "how to look." Nevertheless the chances are that the whole layout and atmosphere of the museum has already given you clearer instructions about how and *what* to see than you realize.

The mere fact that this painting is in a major public gallery has already told you it is "important"—culturally, historically, aesthetically. It is a chosen object, here for you to admire. And it is surrounded, no doubt, by other paintings of the Italian Renaissance: a period defined as "great," a cultural peak in the history of the West, the age that first recaptured the genius of classical antiquity. You are here admiring the painting not just on its own, but also as a symbol of the cultural production of its age. There are, however, other issues that the museum is encouraging you to bear in mind. The paintings are arranged in chronological order: you meet four-teenth-century art before fifteenth-century; fifteenth-century art before sixteenth. You are being asked to assign Piero his place in the *development* of art, to consider how far his treatment of, say, perspective marks an "advance" on his predecessors; you are being taught to look at this painting as a representative of the history of artistic style and technique.

What, though, of the subject matter and context? You may already have reacted somewhat differently to Piero's *Baptism* according to your religious beliefs—Christian, atheist, Moslem, Jew. But what happens if you discover (or perhaps the museum label tells you) that this picture was originally part of a church altarpiece, that it was painted to be the backdrop of the most holy Christian ceremonies? What difference does this make to the way you see it? Instantly then, whatever your own beliefs, you understand that another way of looking is possible. This painting was once a focus of *religious* reverence—not just the *cultural* reverence of today's museum visitor. The scene depicted was a central moment of the Christian faith—not just (as it is for many viewers today) a matter for intellectual "decoding" ("Baptism: Christ in center, John the Baptist to the side").

It is not, of course, only *one* more way of looking that is possible. The original viewers may have been no more homogeneous in their attitudes than we are. Some would perhaps have doubted the Christian faith—and have found it hard to feel any sense of devotion here. Others, with their own private conception of Christ, might simply have been disappointed with Piero's version. The options are almost limitless—although necessarily different from most of the options open to the modern museum-goer.

These considerations are not meant to suggest that the original setting and interpretation of a painting is the only "correct" one. After all, we could never accurately recover the original interpretations of Piero's *Baptism;* we can at best only pretend to be fifteenth-century Italians. We have necessarily made our own new contexts and meanings for paintings of this type. The questions that have been raised, however, are meant to suggest that we should reflect much more carefully on how our ways of seeing are determined and how they vary. Why do we see as we do? As was so clear in the controversies over the exhibition of Hispanic art, the context of our viewing *makes a difference:* new contexts produce new ways of seeing; new ways of seeing produce new meanings.

An exhibition at the New York Center for African Art in 1987 set out to challenge some of the way we classify different types of art, and at the same time to reveal the power of museum display in forming our ways of seeing. A prize exhibit was a very cheap, ordinary hunting net from Zaire. It was laid out on its own, on a low platform, under spot-lighting—the kind of treatment usually reserved for the rarest and most precious objects. The questions being posed here were very simple: How do we now classify this net? What happens when we display it as "art" rather than as cheap "artefact"? Is it still an "ordinary" hunting net, or has it been transformed? And if it has been transformed, what has brought about the transformation?

This was, of course, in some senses a "trick"—a trick that obviously worked rather well, as several dealers in tribal art were drawn to inquire from the Center where they might acquire another such marvelous net! But, as the questions suggest, it had an important point in highlighting the arbitrariness of our normal division between "native craft" and "art"; and in showing the power of museum display in creating "Art" out of the most humble object. Different styles of display can entirely change the way we see what we see. Imagine how humble the net would have remained if it had been displayed in a museum case packed full of other pieces of hunting equipment, and with background information on hunting practices among the Zande people.

These issues of status, valuation, and display are not restricted to the problems of tribal art/craft. They have a much wider resonance in many different areas of the visual arts. Consider, for example, the "masterpieces" of ancient Greek ceramics—the painted vases produced largely in Athens between the sixth and fourth centuries B.C.E., elegantly decorated with scenes drawn from Greek myth and everyday life. These vases are now treated as major works of art: their painters (who sometimes signed their pieces) are discussed by scholars in much the same terms as the painters of the Italian Renaissance; the stylistic details of the painting are minutely compared from vase to vase, influence and imitation from one to another carefully detected; individual vases are given spot-lit, star treatment in most museums. Paradoxically, though, in the ancient world itself the production of these ceramics was a low-grade "craft" activity. Unlike their renowned sculptors or painters on wood or canvas, the men who decorated these vases were, to the Greeks, craftsmen, not artists.

There are various reasons why we have come to value these vase paintings so highly—and so differently from the society that created them. Perhaps the most obvious lies in the accidents of survival: none of the major Greek paintings on wood have survived—we know of them only through the descriptions given by ancient writers; if we want to get any idea of the character of Greek painting, we are *forced* to concentrate on (and so in the process over-value) these paintings on vases. But others might argue that our modern appreciation of these objects as "art" is in fact a proper revaluation of their quality—that the Greeks themselves, in thinking of them as mundane "craft," quite simply failed to recognize their artistic genius. Whatever the underlying reasons, though, it is clear that the modern display of these objects in museums (pride of place in the museum case, shining spotlights onto a single prize specimen) serves to reinforce their high status. The way they are displayed (and so the way that we see them) makes them seem self-evidently "Art."

Could we reverse that valuation? If we consistently displayed these objects in a different way, would we start to think differently about them? Imagine how it would be if they were shown in the case piled one upon another, as if in a cheap china store—not single objects for our admiration. What if we changed their labels and called them "pots," not "vases"? What if we surrounded them with information not about their "artists" or their "painterly technique," but about their domestic use, or about the pottery "industry" in ancient Athens? These changes would, of course, be "tricks," like the "trick" of the Zaire hunting net. But they are tricks that would almost certainly work in making us think quite differently about the objects on display. We would find that we had quite different things to say about these vases or pots, a quite different sense of their value. That in itself should reveal to us how fragile and how variable our judgment of visual objects is.

Explicit conflicts about *how to look* are rare. In other words, the rules we intuit for processing what we see usually do their job very well; they veil from us the sometimes arbitrary, sometimes very loaded choices that we make in classifying and judging the visual world. So, for example, the political agenda that underlies the term "women's craft" or "native craft" (rather than "women's *art*" or "black *art*") is something that most of the time, for most of us, passes unnoticed. But thinking about such conflicts, when they do become explicit, can help to make us aware of the choices that we (or someone on our behalf) are always, necessarily, making when we think about, describe, classify, and *view* works of art.

Earl Miner

Periods and Ideologies

*It is useful to have the categories of "period," "move-
ment," "age," and "generation" to describe literature.
But it is also critical when reading world literature to
understand that each period—and even the term "literature" itself—is an elastic term created by a time, a
place, and an ideology. There is no literary period (for
example, Middle Ages, eighteenth century, Romantic,
Victorian) or genre (lyric, dramatic, narrative) that
does not emerge from the ideology of a particular
culture at a particular time. Each is, therefore, defined
and categorized differently in different cultures.*

Literary periods and their ideologies are easier to assume than explain.
Obviously, to live is to exist in one time and place but not another. It is
not obvious how to define one time or one place. It is reasonable to assume
that our definitions depend on our culture, our interests, and our needs:
the bases of ideology.

"One time" is not fixed in meaning, except that it is somebody's *now*,
somebody's present. The time is shared with others living then but not
with others in a contrasting past or future. Our parents and ancestors lived
before us. The lives of some of them have overlapped with ours. And there
is a family continuance. That continuance is biological and social, and the
social continuance depends upon many things, including a country and a
language. We presume that our families haven't always lived in the country
where they are now; perhaps some or most ancestors did not know English.
These are crude ways of distinguishing periods in our family histories:
before and after coming to this country; before and after knowing English.
If crude, however, the implications are neither simple nor obvious. Especially for *literary* history and its periods.[1]

Anne Dudley Bradstreet (1612-1672) may serve as an example. She
is often called the first American poet. But she thought she was English:
the Declaration of Independence was not signed until over a century after

her death. On the other hand, W.H. Auden and Christopher Isherwood have lived in the United States during this century; they are considered literary figures. Yet they are said to belong to English, not American literature. And the Canadians, Mexicans, and others have their ideas about what "American" may mean.

The established periods of English literature are inconsistently distinguished. The first defies logic, being the "Middle Ages." That first age singular is middle and plural. Later we hear of eighteenth-century, Romantic, Victorian, and modern periods. The bases of distinction differ. The first is a century. "Romantic" is based on certain presumed qualities. "Victorian" is based on a queen. "Modern" comes from Latin for "lately" or "just now," and it was once associated with what was new. (New College, Oxford, was founded, was new or modern, in the fourteenth century.)

Some people have despaired over these inconsistencies. Their remedy is the "neutral" one of centuries—away with "medieval" and "Victorian"! But there is no ideology-free concept of a literary or other period. Our concept of centuries is based on hundred-year periods following the birth of the central figure of one religion. Jews have protested "B.C.," or "before Christ," as a way of designating their history. So we now have "B.C.E.," "before the common era," and "C.E.," or "common era," to replace "A.D.," "anno Domini," "year of Our Lord," The relevance of this revised version is not clear when applied to the vast majority of humankind: ancient Egyptians and Islam; the peoples of India; the Chinese and Japanese. And what about, say, using the Chinese system? They suppose that literature changes with the institution of a dynasty: for example, Tang, Song (Sung), Ming, Quing (Ch'ing). The system has an internal consistency that English literary periods do not. But its relevance outside China is as minimal as B.C.-A.D. is outside Christendom.

A chapter on "Literary History" begins, "Is it *possible* to write literary history . . .?"[2] Clearly, literary history and its periods are concepts, and literature itself is a kind of knowledge. The connection between *what* we know about and our knowledge about that is a hard one to define.[3] There are many, many difficulties in distinguishing literature, histories, and literary histories: If literary history requires full agreement about schemes and principles of periods, then literary history is impossible.

If that were all that had to be considered, the situation would be simple. But in fact it is even less possible *not* to think and talk in literary-historical terms than it is to do so. One reason is simple enough. For many purposes, an entire literature, such as English, is too much to bear in mind at one time and all of it is not relevant anyway. On the other hand, isolated ideas about an individual poet, an individual poem, or a single line are of little use for many purposes. All is too much and one is too little. Groupings by similarity are more typically useful: hence the usefulness of periods, movement, ages, generations, and so on. Hence also the usefulness of other distinctions: lyric, drama, and narrative, or narrative poetry, romance and novel, or, to follow Japanese terms, *monogatari, gesaku,* and *shōsetsu*. Yet those who know the usual implications of the three English and three Japanese terms know that they do not correspond except in being kinds of narrative. Indeed, there is often disagreement whether, say, Hawthorne's *The Scarlet Letter* is a romance or a novel. Some wish to draw rigid distinctions between the two kinds, others to emphasize what they share. Japanese *shōsetsu* are often referred to in English as novels, and *Amerika no shōsetsu* means "the American novel" in Japanese. Or does it, really?

It should be clear that these many necessary but slippery concepts rest on various needs, conceptions, interests, and so on that we may term ideologies.[4] The concept of "ideology" has changed over the years;[5] Its modern meanings originated in Marxist thought and from there passed into usage in the social sciences.[6] The meanings were basically negative: ideology was the motivation of prejudiced, socially wrong, and otherwise mistaken minds. Essentially, ideology was what afflicted *other* people who think wrongly (differently) about social, cultural, and in a word, historical matters.

That traditional concept is obviously illogical. Marxism (or some school or other of the social sciences) is as "other" to those disagreeing with it as those "mistaken minds" are to Marxism. Since name-calling is not productive, we must assume that everybody, ourselves included, is ideologically motivated. We can then redefine ideology: the ideas, values and interests that sometimes contradict, but usually complexly reinforce, each other and that motivate our thought and our conduct. This concept of ideology has won increasing acceptance. In fact, ideological likeness and difference have, in turn, become bases for distinguishing literary periods.[7]

The basic assumption about literary periods today was set forth some years ago: a literary period is distinguished by certain dominant and certain lesser, or dominated, features. The lesser may be those that were dominant in the preceding period (say, religion) or may be new in one period but destined to grow and dominate the next period (say, secularism).[8] Such a principle is easily enough stated. In practice, however, there are difficult questions.

The most basic problem is that "history" has two principal meanings.[9] There is prime history, events occurring. Then there is history as knowledge about the prime history. Prime history is taken to have occurred in a real world to real people in real time and place. That prime history lacks periods, tendencies, meanings, and so on. It is *occurrence* rather than *knowledge*, and so lacks ideology. In practice, however, when we say "history" we usually assume (ideologically) that our knowledge *about* prime history is accurate, identical to it. For most things passing as "histories," the history-as-knowledge is far from history-as-event. Histories are not normally founded in any direct sense on events but on previous writings reshaped by new ideological concerns. (There are no histories of solely oral literatures, for example.)

We do well to recognize that each of us is a historian. And that each of us is enabled and controlled by ideologies. In those terms, we have no choice. But we may be better or worse historians, more or less doctrinaire ideologues. For example, if we undertake a historical argument, we can examine (and declare) our method, our principles. In recent years, however, there seem to have been few full-scale literary histories that have attended to periodizing, ideology, and other matters of method.[10] That is regrettable, because the value to others of knowing the grounds of what we do is small compared to the value to ourselves of so knowing.

These issues are crucial in a *World Reader*. The history, religion art, and social and economic elements in history are less a part of "background"—as if a theatrical set—than of ideology, the reasons according to which people justify. Take a specific issue: the genesis and development of systematic ideas about literature.[11] Only Western literature was defined (by Aristotle) out of drama. All other systematic views of literature were defined out of lyric or (as with the Indian) emerged as if lyric-based. To assume certain things, is therefore, ideologically perverse. It is Western alone to assume that literature is by nature mimetic, fictional; that plot and closure deserve prime attention; that originality is a prime value; that drama and narrative are superior to lyric.

To many of us today, the novel is the characteristic, normal and essential example of what is literary. But the novel is a recent invention. And to read sections of this *Reader* supposing lyric to be anything other than the principal literary genre is to be ideologically perverse.

Of course it is impossible for us wholly to transcend ideologies. We *can* try to identify our ideological presumptions. And we can try to make adequate comparisons.[12] The scale a comparison involves is crucial. English novels seem to differ greatly from Defoe to the latest example. But English novels of the eighteenth century resemble each other more than they do novels of the late twentieth century. As a class of comparison, English novels seem very alike when compared to Russian. The Chinese *xiaoshuo* (vernacular literary prose narrative) differs between the sixteenth and twentieth centuries, but examples look very much alike when compared to the English novel. On the other hand, the *xiaoshuo* may resemble western vernacular prose narrative or novels when compared to lyrics. Of course, we must bear in mind the ideological significance of the "Chinese-ness" or "Englishness" of a narrative.

What can be done besides recognizing our ideological makeups and insuring adequate comparison? It would be foolish to try to invent a whole new periodizing of English literature. We not only use our histories; we are used by them. Clearly, we can regard any period concept as provisional—one among others. That means we should try to avoid the pretense that literature is necessarily and timelessly of a certain kind. Even "literature" itself is an elastic term, swelling or contracting in its given history. Its counterparts (for example, Indian *kavya* or Chinese *wen*) also have their histories. It is a mistake to assume that the meanings of "literature," "*kavya*" and "*wen*" are identical. Three people speaking of "the nineteenth-century realistic novel" may have different "canons," or bodies of defining works in mind.[13] One may be thinking of the novel (*roman, Roman*) in three countries, and the other two may only have England in mind. One may focus on female writers, and the other may be thinking of children as the intended audience. Once again, we owe clarity to ourselves if we are to be clear to others.

In thinking of periods and ideologies, one certainly wishes we had better tools. But we don't, and the tools differ from age to age and country to country. We must use them as appropriately and as well as we can.

NOTES

1. Alexander Dutu, "The Individuation of the Imaginary Universe and the Reconstitution of Literary Periods," in Mario J. Valdés, et al., eds., *Comparative Literary History as Discourse* (Bern: Peter Lang, 1992).

2. René Wellek and Austin Warren, eds., *Theory of Literature* (New York: Harcourt, Brace, 1949), p. 263; see also David Perkins, *Is Literary History Possible?* (Baltimore: Johns Hopkins, 1992).

3. For a general discussion of theory of knowledge, or epistemology, see A. J. Ayer, *The Problem of Knowledge* (London: Macmillan, 1956).

4. See Sacvan Berkovitch and Myra Jehlen, eds., *Ideology and American Literature* (New York: Cambridge Univ. Press, 1986).

5. See Raymond Williams, *Keywords*, rev. ed. (New York: Oxford University Press, 1985).

6. See Edward Shils and Henry M. Johnson (separate articles) in David Shils et al., eds., *International Encyclopedia of the Social Sciences*, vol. 7 (New York: Macmillan and Free Press, 1961); See also Terry Eagleton, *The Ideology of the Aesthetic* (Cambridge: Basil Blackwell, 1990).

7. See Michel Foucault, *The Archaeology of Knowledge and the Discourse on Language*, trans. A. M. Sheridan Smith (New York: Vintage, 1973), see also Timothy J. Reiss, *Tragedy and Truth: Studies in the Development of Renaissance and Neoclassical Discourse* (New Haven: Yale University Press, 1971).

8. Claudio Guillén, *Literature as Style: Essays Toward the Theory of Literary History* (Princeton: Princeton University Press, 1971), p. 435.

9. Earl Miner, "Milton and the Histories," in Kevin Sharpe and Steven N. Zwicker, eds., *Politics of Discourse* (Berkeley and Los Angeles: University of California Press, 1987).

10. See Jin'ichi Konishi, *A History of Japanese Literature* (Princeton: Princeton University Press, 1984-1991), for example the General Introduction.

11. Earl Miner, "On the Genesis and Development of Literary Systems," *Critical Inquiry* (1978-1979) 339-53, 553-68.

12. Earl Miner, "Some Theoretical and Methodological Topics for Comparative Literature," *Poetics Today* 8 (1987): 123-49, and "Inventions of Literary Modernism," *Clio* 21 (1991): 1-22.

13. John Guillory, "Canonical and Non-Canonical: A Critique of the Current Debate," *English Literary History* 54 (1987): 483-527.

Marjorie Perloff

Making Room for the Avant-Garde

The meaning of the term "avant-garde" writing has been constructed from linguistic, political, and social conflict. Originally, "avant-garde" referred not just to artists who were part of a movement considered to be on the cutting edge (futurism, Dada, surrealism), but to the political "advance guard," those who made way for social change. In the latter twentieth century, the meaning of the term "avant-garde" and social and linguistic renewal themselves may be dependent less upon our attention to subject matter than upon the language of experimental writers.

What is the avant-garde? Open any newspaper and you will see ads for "avant-garde" fashions or "avant-garde" restaurants or even "avant-garde" sports equipment. "Avant-garde" in this context usually means "state-of-the-art," the latest thing, the newest, the far-out. And so, when it comes to literature, we still refer to writing that is new and different, writing that is not easily absorbable into the familiar and the traditional, as "avant-garde," even though many critics and social commentators today would argue that there is no longer such a thing as the avant-garde, that, on the contrary, the avant-garde, was a phenomenon of early-twentieth-century European culture, when society and therefore the arts underwent a genuine transformation. Today, these critics would argue, when, at least in the industrialized nations, so much of our thinking is controlled by the media, and when the economy operates so as to neutralize the "new" almost instantly, absorbing it into the larger network of commodity culture, that the "shock of the new," as Robert Hughes called it in his eponymous book, is immediately dissipated.

Originally a French term (and French was for more than a century considered *the* avant-garde literature), *avant-garde* is defined in the *Petit Robert* dictionary as "that part of the army that marches at the head (*en avant*) of the troops." It is important to remember this military derivation of the term—a term that came into being in the wake of the French Revolution—for the *avant-garde* originally referred, not just to artists, but to the political advance-guard, those who paved the way for revolution and social change. That meaning hung on until the late nineteenth century: avant-gardists wanted, not just or even primarily to change artistic and literary production, but to change the world. Only after World War I— when it began to appear that artistic and social/political revolution do not necessarily go hand in hand, that indeed political "revolutionaries" such as the Russian Communists were often very retrograde when it came to the arts and that, vice versa, aesthetic innovation could and did go hand in hand with proto-Fascism, as it did in the work of the Italian futurists and the English vorticists (Ezra Pound, Wyndham Lewis)[1]—did the term "*avant-garde*" begin to be limited to the arts. And today, when the word "art" refers to *haute cuisine* as well as painting, to the creation of computer graphics as well as the composition of sonnets, it is not surprising that our discourse is studded with references to driving an avant-garde car or having an avant-garde haircut.

The consensus is that the great avant-garde movements of Europe (and, to a lesser extent, of the United States and Latin America) occurred in the first two decades of the twentieth century. When the Italian writer F.T. Marinetti published, on the front page of the French newspaper *Le Figaro* his *Futurist Manifesto* (1909), announcing that "We will destroy the museums, libraries, academies of every kind," and instead "will sing of great crowds excited by work, by pleasure, and by revolt," the public sat up and took notice. The technological transformation and urbanization of society—the invention of the automobile, the high-speed train, the telegraph, and especially the airplane—seemed to spell the coming into being of a Brave New World. Such transformation was most notable in hitherto underdeveloped countries like turn-of-the-century Italy and Russia. In the latter, the period between the abortive Revolution of 1905 and the successful Bolshevik Revolution of 1917 proved to be one of the great moments of the avant-garde, producing such famous works as Tatlin's "Tower" (*The Monument to the Third International*), Malevich's *Black Square* paintings, and the *zaum* ("trans-sense") poetry of Khlebnikov and Kruschenyk. It is as if the avant-garde, the front flank of the "army," felt compelled to make up for centuries of torpor and backwardness, compelled to charge into the unknown future head-on.

Then, too, the avant-garde was essentially a group phenomenon: Italian and Russian futurism and German expressionism were followed by the most avant-garde movement of all: Dada. Unlike the futurists, the Dadaists did not extol the machine and the coming of great crowds; on the contrary, the Dadaists, who came of age at the outbreak of World War I (1914), wanted to create art forms that would oppose and challenge the status quo of modern industrial power, a power that had produced war. The artist who was perhaps the most radical avant-gardist of all, Marcel Duchamp, invented an art form called the "readymade." Having come to New York during the war, he bought a urinal at a hardware store, turned it upside down, labeled it "*Fountain* by R. Mutt," and submitted it as an entry in an art exhibition. *Fountain* caused great public consternation but soon ended up in the museum; today, Duchamp's readymades—the urinal, a bottle rack, a bicycle wheel, a bird cage filled with sugar cubes called *Why Not Sneeze, Rrose Sélavy?*—are in museums all over the world. Meanwhile in Paris, Dada soon shaded into surrealism (the search for a hyper-reality, a reality beyond life), a movement founded in the early 1920s by André Breton, which was to be the most international and intermedia avant-garde of all—surrealist film and theatre, poetry and painting, playing a central role in Spain, Latin America, and the United States for decades to come.

One of the interesting and puzzling facets of the avant-garde is that, although everyone agrees that the avant-garde is a group phenomenon, some of the greatest avant-gardists have been isolated individuals, who shunned group identity and struck out on their own. Gertrude Stein, for example, was at least half a century ahead of her time (and she is still ahead of her time) in her creation of verbal compositions using repetition of key word groups and nongrammatical sentences so as to make us see language in an entirely new way. Her famous early book, *Tender Buttons* (1914), for example, takes simple domestic objects—a hat, a pillow, a glass of milk, a carafe of wine—and totally recreates them, as in a cubist painting. Some of the compositions in *Tender Buttons* are very short, like the piece called "ROAST POTATOES," which has only three words:

Roast potatoes for.

This may seem to be no more than a hoax, but think of this little sentence's possible meanings. Stein takes an ordinary potato, a staple of life and "makes it new." "Roast," to begin with, may be an imperative verb (for example, "Roast the potatoes!") or an adjective describing the kind of potatoes to be served. Either way, we can complete the prepositional phrase "for . . ." in various ways: "Roast potatoes for dinner," "Roast potatoes for me," "Roast potatoes for the guests," and so on. Furthermore, "for" is a pun on "four": there are, perhaps, four roast potatoes here. But *four* is also French for "oven" so we have "Roast potatoes [au] four," that is, "baked in the oven."

The plot thickens when we read "Roast potatoes for" in the context of the two little prose poems that precede it:

POTATOES

real potatoes cut in between.

POTATOES

in the preparation of cheese, in the preparation of
crackers, in the preparation of butter, in it.

Not only can potatoes be "cut in between" other vegetables or themselves sliced and stuffed, say, with cheese, but the three potato poems are "cut in between" the other "tender buttons" in Stein's sequence. Further: "cut in between" suggests some sort of relationship with cheese and crackers and butter in the next poem.

Gertrude Stein was an oppositional writer in almost every way possible. She was born in Allegheny, Pennsylvania, of Jewish-immigrant parents, raised in Oakland, California (a town that she later dismissed with the words, "There is no there there"), and became an American expatriate living in Paris. As a woman writer at a time when women writers were marginalized, and as a lesbian writer at a time when American society was overtly homophobic, she could never really fit into any group, regularly refusing categories like "woman writer," "homosexual writer," "Jewish-American writer," and so on. But today Stein is recognized as, in her own words, "The Mother of Us All," exerting a profound influence on young poets, fiction writers, playwrights, and critics. She was, in the most literal sense, avant-garde.

Let us now turn to a related question: How is the "avant-garde" to be represented in an anthology like the *HarperCollins World Reader?* Aren't anthologies by definition collections of writings that represent the status quo? After all, an anthology like this one is put together for college students by an Establishment publishing company, and the editors and professors who plan the project, make the selections, and put the book into production are themselves evidently established and respected scholars who have succeeded in the professional world. Reading a heavy book like the *HarperCollins World Reader* in a college course, perhaps even a required course, would seem to be about as far away as one can get from the notion of the avant-garde as front-runners of the army, from the notion, say, of the Dada group at the Cabaret Voltaire in Zurich, wearing wild costumes and makeup and declaiming as did Hugo Ball in 1916, a "Sound poem" called "Karawne" that begins:

> gadji beri bimba gladridi laula lonni cadori
> gadjama gramma berida bimbala glandri glassassa
> lautialomini . . .

Then, too, as the contemporary American avant-garde poet David Antin put it during one of his performances, "Anthologies are to poets as the zoo is to animals," meaning that the very act of anthologizing, of making selections from a writer's whole *oeuvre*, of picking *X* rather than *Y*, and only one chapter of *X* at that, is a kind of straightjacket, forcing the writer into a "cage" he or she never wanted to be in.

There is no use denying that anthologizing is thus an enormous problem, especially when it comes to avant-garde writing. Anthologies designed for college classrooms have tended to be cautious, preferring to confine themselves to the tried and true. When I was a freshman, the very look of the heavyweight anthology we were using was enough to turn me off, and certainly the anthology was considered the last place in the world where one would find exciting, off-beat, contemporary, avant-garde writing.

Those who put together the *HarperCollins World Reader* were, I think, acutely aware of this problem. At the same time, we have to recognize that one of the great inventions of the twentieth century has been the "alternative" anthology, an anthology that comes into existence precisely in order to shake up our "anthology-speak" and make us aware of other models. The poet Jerome Rothenberg, for example, has over the past few decades put together anthologies such as *Shaking the Pumpkin*, which focuses on native American poetry, *Revolution of the Word*, which contains little-known Dada and surrealist works juxtaposed to postmodern American texts, and, with George Quasha, *America A Prophecy*, which ranges over an enormous body of material from ancient epic to Dada to postmodern experimental texts by "ethno-poets" like Rothenberg himself.

Such anthologies are avant-garde in that they introduce us to new ways of framing or contextualizing material that we all know. In the section of *America A Prophecy* called "Visions," for example, a fragment from Walt Whitman's "The Sleepers" ("Pier that I saw dimly last night when I looked from the windows. . . ") is preceded by a version of the "Hehaka Sapa" ("The Dog Vision," by the Oglala Sioux "holy man" known as Black Elk ("Standing in the center of the sacred place and facing the sunset, I began to cry"). The Whitman poem is, in turn, followed by a selection from a nineteenth-century account of hashish visions by Fitzhugh Ludlow, and then by Emily Dickinson's "I Think I Was Enchanted," which ends with the stanza:

> To Tomes of solid Witchcraft—
> Magicians be asleep—
> But Magic—hath an Element
> Like Deity—to keep—

The conjunction of four such different visions has a startling effect: "Witchcraft," for example, takes on many shades of meaning and relationship of "Magic" to "Deity," made explicit in Dickinson's poem and central to the Sioux "Dog Vision" and Ludlow's "The Hasheesh Eater," is also an issue in Whitman's seemingly secular "The Sleepers."

In the *World Reader* you will find similar conjunctions, even though the arrangement is chronological and the literary texts are generally grouped by nation or culture. But not only are the juxtapositions of, say, fourteenth-century Korean lyric (Hwang Hŭí, "Spring has come to a country village") and medieval Latin poetry startling, but to read, say, such West African poems as Gabriel Okara's "You Laughed and Laughed and Laughed" (1978) against contemporary experimental poems produced in the United States and Canada is to learn that "making it new" has become a genuinely global project.

A key figure in this new "globalist" avant-garde is the great black Caribbean poet Aimé Césaire, whose language is French. Césaire's biography (he celebrated his eightieth birthday in 1993) intersects with most of major poetry currents of his time. Born the son of a local tax inspector in Basse-Pointe, a small town on the northeast coast of Martinique, Césaire won entrance to the Lycée Louis-le-Grand in Paris when he was eighteen and remained in France until 1944, studying at the illustrious Ecole Normale Supérieure and beginning to make his way as a writer. His poetry fuses French surrealism, ethnography, African-American "primitivism," as derived from the Harlem Renaissance poet with whose work he came into contact in Paris, and the concept of "négritude," which he developed together with Senegalese poet Leopold Senghor. An avid student of Nietzsche, a lover of Rimbaud and Mallarmé, Césaire was also intensely political. When he returned to Martinique after World War II, he ran on the Communist party ticket and was elected mayor; in this capacity, he was soon sent as a delegate to Paris to participate in the drafting of a new constitution for the Fourth Republic. "I joined the Communist party," wrote Césaire, "because, in a world not yet cured of racism, where the fierce exploitation of colonial populations still persists, the Communist party embodies the will to work effectively for the coming of the only social and political order we can accept—because it will be founded on the right of all men to dignity without regard to origin, religion, or color."[1] If this call for social justice uncannily foreshadows the political discourse of some of our own black leaders, it is also important to mention that Césaire left the Communist party in 1956 when Soviet troops invaded Hungary. Disillusioned with communism, he became the leader of the independent socialist Progressive Party of Martinique (PPM) and served in political office until his retirement.

What makes Césaire's poetry so important for the works we call "avant-garde"? Works such as the long prose poem *Notebook of a Return to the Native Land* (1947) provide an explosive account of what it means to be a black man in a white man's world. Self-recognition has to precede revolutionary text and action. The reaction of avant-garde writing stems from linguistic as well as social conflict. Césaire never sentimentalizes this situation. Nothing earns his hatred as much of some of his abject countrymen, for example, the *nègre* he meets one evening on the streetcar:

A nigger big as a pongo trying to make himself small on the streetcar bench. He was trying to leave behind, on this grimy bench, his gigantic legs and his trembling famished boxer hands. And everything had left him, was leaving him. His nose which looked like a drifting peninsula and even his negritude discolored as a result of untiring tawing. And the tawer was Poverty. A big unexpected lop-eared bat whose claw marks in his face had scabbed over into crusty islands. Or rather, it was a tireless worker Poverty was, working on some hideous cartouche. One could easily see how that industrious and malevolent thumb had kneaded bumps into his brow, bored two bizarre parallel tunnels in his nose, overexaggerated his lips, and in a masterpiece of caricature, planed, polished and varnished the tiniest cutest little ear in all creation. . . .

He was COMICAL and UGLY
COMICAL AND UGLY for sure
I displayed a big complicitous smile. . . .

This description is remarkable for its savagery and grotesquerie, its mix of indignation and sardonic humor. Throughout *Notebook*, Césaire demonstrates his astonishing learning—his knowledge, for example, of his island's flora and fauna, of local cannibal myths and voodoo—fused with racy, concrete, immediate, idiomatic speech and a visionary drive toward transcendence. The mixture of modes encourages this self-realization. The poet is as hard on himself as on his fellow Martinicans, blaming their condition not on some abstract "Them," but on the terrible complexities of the colonial situation—a situation that had also, after all, brought him into contact with the poetry he most loved, that of French symbolism and surrealism.

If we turn from *Notebook of a Return to the Native Land* to the poems in the American Modernist section of the *World Reader*, something startling happens. The nature imagery of, say, Robert Frost may seem "modernist" in relationship to traditional American poetry, but suppose we read Frost's "Birches" against the following passage from Césaire's *Notebook of a Return to the Native Land*:

> Tepid dawn of ancestral heat and fears
> overboard with alien riches
> overboard with my genuine falsehoods
> But what strange pride suddenly illuminates me!
> let the hummingbird come
> let the sparrow hawk come
> let the breach in the horizon
> the cynocephalus
> let the lotus bearer of the world come
> the pearly upheaval of dolphins
> cracking the shell of the sea
> let a plunge of islands come. . . .

>let the ovaries of the water come where the future
>   stirs the testicles
>let the wolves come who feed in the untamed
>   openings of the body at the hour when my
>moon and your sun meet at the ecliptic inn. . . .

Here the strangeness of the imagery, in part derived from surrealism but also derived from Césaire's native tradition, clearly has more in common with the work of postmodernist American poets like James Merrill or John Ashbery than with poets labeled as "Modernist" in histories of American literature. Césaire's poetry is thus avant-garde in that his writing in the 1930s and 1940s set the stage for what was to come decades later in Anglo-America.

Why not sooner? Perhaps because the creation of avant-garde writing as we have already claimed, comes out of linguistic as well as social conflict. Césaire's native language was creole (an oral vernacular), but the family's middle-class aspirations were such that he was taught "proper" French as a child and introduced to the French classics. Indeed, French was the only written language an educated Martinican would have known. Accordingly, when Césaire came to Paris he adopted two roles: that of the difficult, sophisticated highly literary surrealist poet, and that of the outspoken opponent of racial oppression. In his late guise, Césaire, was of course, closer to the writers of the Harlem Renaissance than to André Breton or Louis Aragon. Yet ironically, the largely straightforward, realistic narratives of Claude McKay and Jean Toomer struck Césaire as excessively bourgeois. Having tasted the pleasures of the text—where text refers to a difficult, intricate form of writing that foregrounds language at the expense of character and plot—he could hardly begin to write like Langston Hughes or Countee Cullen. Complexly waged politics, the fight for racial equality, the battle against oppression—these would have to be stated indirectly. The result is a clotted language, "elitist" in its disregard for the reader, using as it does obscure botanical and zoological terms, creole dialect, elaborate punning, mythological reference, and so on.

Césaire's trajectory is thus rather different from that of Claude Mckay, Jean Toomer, and later, Ralph Ellison and Toni Morrison, writers who are not usually labeled "avant-garde." Indeed, minority writing in the United States has generally tended to be anti-avant-garde. African-American, Asian-American, Chicano, gay and lesbian literatures—all these, at least in their more popular forms, have emphasized subject matter, ready communicability, direct impact, a kind of "Go for the burn!" mentality, rather than indirection and verbal complexity. Language, so the argument of our own minority discourse goes, should not be "privileged," at least not at the expense of the communication of a specific political message.

The resulting literary situation is curious. Does "marginalization," a term we currently hear a great deal about, refer to representative marginalization (for example, Writer X "represents" the African-American mentality), or the quite literal marginalization of those writers devoted to their craft who nevertheless fail to get recognition because of the strangeness and difficulty of their work? If, that is to say, Toni Morrison is "marginalized," how is it that she regularly appears on TV talk shows, gives interviews, and makes the best-seller lists? Or again, if Morrison is marginalized, where do we place a black writer like Bob Kaufman, whose jazz poems are still largely unknown except to a small, devoted coterie of like-minded poets?

The battle over the role of language in literature has by no means been resolved: witness the avant-garde grouping known as "language poetry." The label has caused the poets in question much difficulty, its implication being that other poets somehow don't pay attention to language. But what the poets in question—Bruce Andrews, Rae Armantrout, Charles Bernstein, Lyn Hejinian, Susan Howe, Steve McCaffery, Bob Perelman, and Ron Silliman, to mention only a few—have meant by the label is that poetry must once again claim its rightful position as the art form that foregrounds language in all its materiality. Poetry, they argue, is not some sort of message or cry from the heart, first experienced and *then* embodied in suitable language but on the contrary: "When words are, meaning soon follows," to quote Ron Silliman; or, as Lyn Hejinian put it, "Where once one sought a vocabulary for ideas, now one seeks ideas for vocabularies."[2]

What these poets imply is that in a world as heavily mediaized as ours, a world where formulaic phrases and sentences permeate public discourse, poetry must begin with the words actually used in everyday life and renew them by transforming the syntactic formations and contexts in which they occur, forcing us to think through their implications. Strange as the resulting poetry may seem to readers accustomed to, say, the more imagistic lyric of a Gary Snyder, it makes perfect sense when read against Gertrude Stein's *Tender Buttons* or Aimé Césaire's *Notebook of a Return to the Native Land.*

In his encyclopedic, brilliantly playful and punning *The Martyrology*, for example, the Canadian poet bpNichol, whose linguistic experiments predate "language poetry," explores the music of language in all its poten-tial. A postmodern version of the religious quest poem, *The Martyrology* introduces the reader to the poet's saints—the saints, we might say, of everyday life. Gertrude Stein, for example, is reincarnated here via a pun as "St. Ein." "The Grammar Trilogy" (1987) begins as follows:

bio
       graphy
geo
                  writing a self
                        a country
      landscape a can be in
                        clOud
                        cl ud
                              (or, as in that poem I never published
                              (not knowing the etymology):
                        CLOUD
                           O
                           O
                           O
                        STONE
                              too much the clod to see it then
                              (ear to the earth))

If this extract looks like one of Marinetti's *Parole in Libertà,* it is in fact quite different. Nichol's interest is not in drawing analogies between disparate nouns but in taking language itself apart and seeing how it works—a very postmodern preoccupation. Take the *O* out of "clOud" and you have a "cl ud" that becomes "included" if we add it to the previous line. Take the *U* out of "cloUd," and you're left with "clod" ("too much the clod to see it then"). And further: a "cloud" in the sky parallels a "stone" on the ground, for both center the letter *O* between two letters (left) and two letters (right). Be careful, Nichol seems to be telling us, not to take anything for granted. Language is never just a conduit to a meaning outside and beyond it.

A similar faith animates the radical poetics of Susan Howe, but hers is less autobiographical, more historical and cultural than bpNichols's and she is also writing from a specifically feminist point of view. In a poetic sequence like *Melville's Marginalia,* as well as in such critical texts as *My Emily Dickinson* and *The Birth-mark* (but how do we really tell "poetry" apart from "critical prose," given the prose-verse mix of all these books?),

Howe engages in a profound interrogation of the "outsider" in American and in Anglo-Irish culture, from the captivity narrative of Mary Rowlandson, to the spiritual and mental isolation and genius of Herman Melville and Emily Dickinson, to the failed rebellion of such renegades as the Irish nationalist poet and the Harvard professor-critic F. O. Matthiessen. Howe doesn't write *about* these people and events; rather, she writes what might be called documentary collage, a collage in which the "real" historical material is reproduced, fragmented, and spliced with her own lyric commentary, often in the gnomic form of rebuses and picture-puzzle poems. The result is that "history," though never a "progress," becomes, in the words on one of her best poems, an "articulation of sound forms in time." At the end of the Preface to *Melville's Marginalia*, we read:

> Round about the margin or edge of anything in a way that
> is close to the limit. A narrow margin.   Slightly.
> If water is margined-imagined by the tender grass.
> Marginal.   Belonging to the brink or margent.
> The brink of brim from anything from telepathy to poetry.
> A marginal growth of willow and water flag.
> A feather on the edge of a bird's wing.

Here, as in bpNichol's *Martyrology*, a single word ("*margin*") is taken apart and then sent for the wildest possible sort of spin. It is this attention to language in its tiniest (and yet also potentially largest) manifestations that characterizes the avant-garde in the new global world of the late twentieth century.

NOTES

1.   An English movement relating to the vortex, or whirlpool, of energy at the center of an abstract form, conceived as both still and moving.

2.   Aimé Césaire, cited in Clayton Eshleman and Annette Smith, "Introduction," in *The Collected Poetry of Aimé Césaire*, trans. Clayton Eshleman and Annette Smith (Berkeley, Los Angeles, and London: University of California Press, 1983), p. 4.

3.   Ron Silliman, "For L=A=N=G=U=A=G=E" and Lyn Hejinian, "If Written is Writing," in *The L=A=N=G=U=A=G=E Book*, Bruce Andrews and Charles Bernstein, eds. (Carbondale and Edwardsville: Southern Illinois Press, 1984), pp. 16, 29.

Brief Bibliography

GENERAL

Bakhtin, Mikhail, M. *The Dialogic Imagination*. Edited by Michael Holquist. Translated by Caryl Emerson and Michael Holquist. Austin: University of Texas Press, 1981.

Barthes, Roland. *Critical Essays*. Translated by Richard Howard. Evanston: Northwestern University Press, 1972.

—. *Writing Degree Zero*. Translated by Annette Lavers and Colin Smith. New York: Hill and Wang, 1968.

de Man, Paul. *Allegories of Reading*. New Haven: Yale University Press, 1977.

Derrida, Jacques. "The Violence of the Letter: From Lévi-Strauss to Rousseau." In *Of Grammatology*, translated by Gayatri Chakravorty Spivak, 101-140. Baltimore and London: Johns Hopkins University Press, 1974.

—. "Structure, Sign and Play." In *The Structuralist Controversy*, edited by Richard Macksey and Eugenio Donato. Baltimore: Johns Hopkins University Press, 1972.

Eagleton, Terry. *Literary Theory: An Introduction*. Minneapolis: University of Minnesota Press, 1983.

Fish, Stanley. *Is There a Text in this Class?: The Authority of Interpretive Communities*. Cambridge, Mass.: Harvard University Press, 1980.

Foucault, Michel. *The Foucault Reader*. Edited by Paul Rabinow. New York: Pantheon, 1984.

—. *The Order of Things: An Archaeology of the Human Sciences*. Translated by A. M. Sheridan Smith. New York: Vintage Books, 1973.

Geertz, Clifford. *The Interpretation of Cultures*. New York: Basic Books, 1973.

Gallop, Jane. *The Daughter's Seduction: Feminism and Psychoanalysis*. Ithaca: Cornell University Press, 1982.

Groden, Michael and Martin Kreiswirth, eds. *Johns Hopkins Guide to Literary Theory and Criticism*, 1993.

Jameson, Fredric. *Postmodernism or the Cultural Logic of Late Capitalism*. Durham: Duke University Press, 1991.

Harari, José. *Textual Strategies*. Ithaca: Cornell University Press, 1979.

Kristeva, Julia, "Politics and the Polis." In *The Politics of Interpretation*, edited by W. J. T. Mitchell. Chicago: University of Chicago Press, 1983.

Kuhn, Thomas. *The Structure of Scientific Revolution*. Chicago: University of Chicago Press, 1970.

Lentricchia, Frank and Thomas McLaughlin, eds. *Critical Terms for Literary Study*. Chicago: University of Chicago Press, 1985.

Miller, J. Hillis. *The Ethics of Reading*. New York: Columbia University Press, 1987.

Preminger, Alex, ed. *Princeton Encyclopedia of Poetry and Poetics*, 3rd ed., Princeton University Press, 1993.

Tompkins, Jane, ed. *Reader Response Criticism: From Formalism to Post Structuralism*. New York and Oxford: Oxford University Press, 1980.

LITERATURE AND POLITICS

Howe, Irving. *Politics and the Novel.* Cleveland and New York: World Publishers, 1957.

Gates, Henry Louis, Jr., ed. *Race, Writing and Difference*. Chicago: University of Chicago Press, 1986.

Johnson, Barbara. *A World of Difference*. Baltimore: Johns Hopkins University Press, 1987.

Miller, Nancy K., ed. *The Poetics of Gender*. New York: Columbia University Press, 1986.

Mitchell, W. J. T., ed. *The Politics of Interpretation*. Chicago: University of Chicago Press, 1983.

Plato. *The Republic of Plato*. Translated and edited by Francis MacDonald Cornford. Oxford: Oxford University Press, 1941.

Said, Edward W. *The World, the Text, and the Critic*. Cambridge, Mass.: Harvard University Press, 1983.

—. *Orientalism*. New York: Random House, 1979.

Sartre, Jean-Paul. *"What Is Literature? and Other Essays*. Translated by Bernard Frechtman, et al. Cambridge, Mass.: Harvard University Press, 1988.

Spivak, Gayatri Chakravorty. *In Other Worlds: Essays in Cultural Politics*. New York and London: Routledge, 1988.

Suleiman, Susan Rubin. *Authoritarian Fictions: The Ideological Novel as a Literary Genre*. 2nd ed., with a new introduction by the author. Princeton: Princeton University Press, 1992.

—. *Subversive Intent: Gender, Politics, and the Avant-Garde*. Cambridge, Mass.: Harvard University Press, 1990.

SPEAKING AND WRITING

Anderson, Benedict. *Imagined Communities: Reflections on the Origin and Spread of Nationalism*. London and New York: Verso, 1983.

Derrida, Jacques. "The Violence of the Letter: From Lévi-Strauss to Rousseau." In *Of Grammatology*, translated by Gayatri Chakravorty Spivak, 101-140. Baltimore and London: Johns Hopkins University Press, 1976.

Goody, Jack and Ian Watt. "The Consequences of Literacy." in *Literacy in Traditional Societies*, edited by Jack Goody. Cambridge: Cambridge University Press, 1968.

Hirsch, E. D., Jr. *Cultural Literacy: What Every American Needs to Know*. New York: Random House, 1987.

Jones, Gayl. *Liberating Voices: Oral Traditions in African American Literature*. Cambridge: Harvard University Press: 1991.

Kutzinski, Vera. *Against the American Grain: Myth and History in William Carlos Williams, Jay Wright, and Nicolás Guillén*. Chapter Two: "The Black Limbo," 47-130. Baltimore: Johns Hopkins University Press, 1987.

Miller, Christopher L. *Theories of Africans: Anthropology and Literature in Francophone Africa*. Chicago: University of Chicago Press, 1990.

Street, Brian. *Literacy in Theory and Practice*. Cambridge: Cambridge University Press, 1984.

Thompson, Robert Farris. *The Flash of the Spirit*. New York: Random House, 1983.

GENDER

Abel, Elizabeth, ed. *Writing and Sexual Difference*. Chicago: Chicago University Press, 1982.

Auerbach, Nina. *Communities of Woman: An Idea in Fiction.* Cambridge, Mass: Harvard University Press, 1978.

Butler, Judith. *Gender Trouble: Feminism and the Subversion of Identity.* New York and London: Routledge, 1990.

Chow, Rey. *Women and Chinese Modernity.* Minneapolis: University of Minnesota Press, 1991.

Cixous, Hélène. "The Laugh of the Medusa." In *New French Feminisms*, edited by Elaine Marks and Isabelle de Courtivron. Amherst: University of Massachusetts Press, 1980.

de Lauretis, Teresa, ed. *Feminist Studies, Critical Studies.* Bloomington: Indiana University Press, 1986.

Fetterly, Judith. *The Resisting Reader: A Feminist Approach to American Fiction,* Bloomington: Indiana University Press, 1978.

Flynn, Elizabeth A. and Patrocino P. Schweickert, *Gender and Reading: Essays on Readers, Texts, and Contexts.* Baltimore: Johns Hopkins University Press, 1986.

Gilbert, Sandra, and Susan Gubar. *The Madwoman in the Attic: The Woman Writer and the Nineteenth-Century Literary Imagination.* New Haven: Yale University Press, 1979.

Heilbrun, Carolyn. *Hamlet's Mother and Other Essays.* New York: Ballantine, 1990.

—. *Writing a Women's Life.* New York: Norton, 1988.

Jacobus, Mary. "The Difference of View." In *Women Writing and Writing about Women,* edited by Mary Jacobus, 10-21. New York: Harper and Row, 1979.

Kamuf, Peggy. "Replacing Feminist Criticism." *Diacritics,* Summer (1982): 42-47.

Keohane, Nannerel O., Michelle J. Rosaldo, Barbara G. Gelpi, eds. *Feminist Theory: A Critique of Ideology.* Chicago: University of Chicago Press, 1982.

Kolodny, Annette. "Dancing Through the Minefields." In *New Feminist Criticism: Essays on Women, Literature and Theory,* edited by Elaine Showalter. New York: Pantheon, 1985.

McDowell, Deborah E. "New Directions for Black Feminist Criticism." 186-199. In *The New Feminist Criticism,* edited by Elaine Showalter. New York: Pantheon, 1985.

Miller, Nancy K. *Getting Personal.* New York and London: Routledge, 1991.

—. *Subject to Change.* New York: Columbia University Press, 1988.

Rich, Adrienne. "When We Dead Awaken: Writing as Re-vision." *College English* 34 (1972): 18-30.

Showalter, Elaine. "Feminist Criticism in the Wilderness." *Critical Inquiry* 2, 2 (Winter 1981): 179-205. Reprinted in *Writing and Sexual Difference*, edited by Elizabeth Abel, Chicago: University of Chicago Press, 1982.

—, ed. *Feminist Criticism: Essays on Women, Literature,* and *Theory.* New York: Pantheon, 1985.

Stimpson, Catharine R. *Where the Meanings Are: Feminism and Cultural Spaces.* New York and London: Methuen, 1988.

Woolf, Virginia. *A Room of One's Own.* New York: Harcourt, Brace, Jovanovich, 1967.

IDENTITY

Anderson, Benedict. *Imagined Communities: Reflections on the Origin and Spread of Nationalism.* London: Verso, 1983.

Anzaldúa, Gloria. *Borderlands: La Frontera.* San Francisco: Spinsters Ink, 1987.

—. "Speaking in Tongues: A Letter to Third World Women Writers." In *This Bridge Called My Back: Writings by Radical Women of Color,* edited by Cherrie Moraga and Gloria Anzaldúa. New York: Kitchen Table: Women of Color Press, 1983.

Balibar, Etienne and Immanuel Wallerstein. *Race, Nation, Class: Ambiguous Identities.* London: Verso, 1991.

Brennan, Tim. "Cosmopolitans and Celebrities." *Race and Class,* 31:1, July-Sept. 1989, 1-19.

Brownstein, Rachel M. *Becoming a Heroine: Reading About Women in Novels,* New York: Viking, 1982.

Carby, Hazel. *Reconstructing Womanhood.* New York: Oxford University Press, 1987.

Christian, Barbara, ed. *Black Feminist Criticism: Perspectives on Black Women Writers.* New York: Pergamon, 1985.

Deleuze, Gilles and Felix Guattari. "What is a Minor Literature?" *Mississippi Review,* 11 (3): 13-33.

hooks, bell [Gloria Watkins]. *Yearning: Race, Gender and Cultural Politics.* Boston: South End Press, 1990.

Hull, Gloria T., Patricia Bell Scott, Barbara Smith, eds. *All the Women Are White, All the Blacks Are Men, But Some of Us Are Brave: Black Womens' Studies.* Old Westbury: Feminist Press, 1982.

Irigaray, Luce. *Speculum of the Other Woman.* Ithaca, N.Y.: Cornell University Press, 1985.

Ruddick, Sara. *Working It Out.* New York: Pantheon, 1977.

Said, Edward W. "Secular Criticism." In *Critical Theory Since 1965*, Hazard Adams and Leroy Searle, eds., Tallahassee: Florida State University Press, 1986, 605-622.

Smith, Valerie. *Self-discovery and Authority in African-American Narrative.* Cambridge: Harvard University Press, 1987.

Wittig, Monique. "The Straight Mind." *Feminist Issues.* (Summer 1980) (1): 103-112.

HISTORY AND IDEOLOGY

Ayer, A. J., *The Problem of Knowledge.* London: Macmillan, 1956.

Bercovitch, Sacvan, and Myra Jehlen, eds., *Ideology and American Literature.* New York: Cambridge University Press, 1986.

Dutu, Alexandru. "The Individuation of the Imaginary Universe and the Reconstitution of Literary Periods." In *Comparative Literary History as Discourse*, edited by Mario J. Valdés, et al. Bern: Peter Lang, 1992.

Eagleton, Terry. *The Ideology of the Aesthetic.* Cambridge, UK: Basil Blackwell, 1990.

Guillén, Claudio. *Literature as System: Essays Toward the Theory of Literary History.* Princeton: Princeton University Press, 1971.

Guillory, John. "Canonical and Non-canonical: A Critique of the Current Debate." *English Literary History.* 54 (1987): 483-527.

Konishi, Jin'ichi. *A History of Japanese Literature.* Vols. 1-3. Princeton: Princeton University Press, 1984-1991.

Miner, Earl. "That Literature Is a Kind of Knowledge." *Critical Inquiry.* 2 (1976): 487-518.

—. "On the Genesis and Development of Literary Systems." *Critical Inquiry.* 5 (1978-1979).

—. *Comparative Poetics; An Intercultural Essay on Theories.* Princeton. Princeton University Press, 1990.

Perkins, David. *Is Literary History Possible?* Baltimore: Johns Hopkins, 1992.

Reiss, Timothy J. *Tragedy and Truth: Studies in the Development of Renaissance and Neoclassical Discourse.* New Haven: Yale University Press, 1971.

—. *The Discourse of Modernism.* Ithaca: Cornell University Press, 1982.

Sharpe, Kevin and Steven N. Zwicker, eds. *Politics of Discourse.* Berkeley and Los Angeles: University of California Presss, 1987.

Shils, Edward and Henry M. Johnson. "Ideology" (separate articles) in David L. Shils, et al., eds., *International Encyclopedia of the Social Sciences.* Vol. 7. New York: Macmillan and Free Press, 1961.

von Hallberg, Robert, ed. *Canons.* Chicago: University of Chicago Press, 1983.

Wellek, René and Austin Warren. *Theory of Literature.* New York: Harcourt, Brace, 1949.

Williams, Raymond. *Keywords.* Rev. ed. New York: Oxford University Press, 1985.

ART AND LITERATURE

Arnheim, Rudolf. *Visual Thinking.* Berkeley: University of California, 1969.

Berger, John. *Ways of Seeing.* New York: Penguin, 1977.

—. *About Looking.* New York: Pantheon, 1980.

—. *The Sense of Sight.* New York: Pantheon, 1985.

Broude, Norma and Garrard, Mary D. *The Expanding Discourse: Feminism and Art History.* New York: HarperCollins Icon Editions, 1992.

Bryson, Norman. *Vision and Painting: The Logic of the Gaze.* New Haven: Yale University Press, 1983.

Bryson, Norman. *Visual Theory.* New York: HarperCollins Icon Editions, 1993.

Caws, Mary Ann. *The Art of Interference: Stressed Readings in Verbal and Visual Texts.* Princeton: Princeton University Press, 1989.

—. *The Eye in the Text: Essays on Perception, Mannerist to Modern.* Princeton: Princeton University Press, 1972.

Chadwick, Whitney. *Women Artists and the Surrealist Movement.* Boston: Little Brown, 1985.

Mulvey, Laura. *Visual and Other Pleasures.* Bloomington: Indiana University Press, 1989.

Nochlin, Linda. *Women, Art, and Power, and Other Essays.* New York: Harper and Row, 1988.

Stewart, Susan. *On Longing: Narratives of the Miniature, the Gigantic, the Souvenir, the Collection.* Baltimore: Johns Hopkins University Press, 1984.